TRACK CHANGES:
A HANDBOOK FOR ART CRITICISM

Track changes: a handbook for art criticism

PAPER MONUMENT

EDITED BY MIRA DAYAL
AND JOSEPHINE HESTON

INTRODUCTION

INTRODUCTION
MIRA DAYAL

ON HAVING AN AGENDA

Track changes is a collective response to a set of ongoing questions: What makes an art-writing practice or an editorial process feminist? How do critics and editors of color find entry points, guidance, and support in an art world that has long prioritized straight, white, male writers, artists, and readers? How do we decide which artists to uphold or critique, and how do we understand the impact of our critiques? What agendas do writers and editors operate under?

This last question often arises in my work at art publications. When discussing potential contributors with colleagues, I have occasionally heard that a writer seems to "have an agenda," in the sense of an ideology that guides one's behavior. The observation is invariably meant as a criticism: that the writer tends to focus on a specific category of artists, often a historically underrepresented one; that the purpose of their work is primarily to articulate a sociopolitical stance; that they see issues more than artworks; that their work reiterates expected arguments rather than generating different viewpoints.

From an editor's perspective, I can understand the sentiment: a writer's focus on a particular subject could mean that they aren't interested in broader commissions or would only have positive things to say about anything on that subject. From a writer's perspective, I know that having an agenda that sets parameters on what I write about can limit what I seek out or dim my interest in a subject over time.

Yet the label—*has an agenda*—irks me. First, its selective application often implies that writing primarily on, say, white, male, heterosexual, cisgender painters—or those artists and works whose identities and subjects are supposedly unmarked—does *not* count as having an agenda, even though that persistent model is similarly specific, ideological, and consequential. It also sounds like a way to spin *focus* (otherwise thought of as expertise) into a negative attribute when the focus is on subjects deemed less valuable. If this label is intended to turn an editor or reader away from a critic, its effect is often to maintain the field's historical priorities while preventing underrepresented subjects from becoming too prominent.

Second, the critic who "has an agenda" is taken to be compromised, unlike the critic who purports to maintain objective authority through professed neutrality. But the critic has never been neutral in this sense. The field of art criticism was formed through debates over priorities, and since its beginnings it has been bound by many parameters, from gender to genre. Critiquing art requires asking: Under what rubric should art be evaluated? Should formal or moral concerns come first? How important are subjectivity and expression, for the artist and for the writer? What role does the critic play in shaping hierarchies of taste or value? These questions will never be settled, and each critic will have their own answers.

I have thus come to see agendas as fruitful: when defined not only as an ideological program but also as a plan, a conscious set of considerations and objectives, the agenda is essential for the critic. It is a tool for proactively shaping one's editorial practice in order to resist bias and clarify one's position.

Track changes brings together commissioned texts, reprinted essays, and conversational excerpts in which writers and editors discuss their agendas and intentions, as well as the challenges they have faced in publishing. Structured as a handbook, the collection explores how this expanded conception of an agenda plays out at all stages of the writing and editing process, from pitching and commissioning to reading and reflecting. Several contributors have previously published essays outlining their editorial objectives, some have intentionally changed the form of—and audience for—their writing over time, and many have a history of practicing critique with an implied focus. The agendas that emerge from their texts are often intersectional, accounting for how a writer's or artist's gender, race, and sexuality affect the stakes and strictures, and forms and functions, of their work. All the contributors have thus undertaken the types of intentional planning and ideological repositioning that inform this book's definition of the agenda—even if some of them might not identify with the usually negative label of "having an agenda." Taken together, these texts constitute a guide to the field of art criticism from the perspective of those actively shaping it.

One motivating principle of *Track changes* is that, in art criticism, small decisions and added voices have a cumulative effect—and given that criticism touches all other parts of the art world, including the school, studio, market, and museum, writing can shape the focus, tone, and politics of the larger field. Commissioning a more diverse set of writers to cover a broader range of artists is just the starting point in redressing inequities in the field. We imagine here what a more concerted strategy might look like, what kinds of relations and reconfigurations our agendas could achieve.

SHAPING THE DECISION TREE

Writing, editing, and publishing require multiple stages of nuanced considerations, not all of which are apparent in the final texts. How does a writer or editor choose which artists to address or which themes to focus on? Why does a writer choose a certain vocabulary, or make specific comparisons, within their texts? How does an editor provide feedback to a writer, and what kinds of conversations happen within the comment boxes? How do editors shape their relationships with writers? How does a writer shift their priorities over the course of their career? Since much of this is worked out behind the scenes, before a text is published, it is difficult for a reader to recognize the critic's subjectivity and the criteria that inform their decisions. This is compounded by the fact that editorial work is often framed as self-effacing: one sign of a good editor is their ability to more clearly articulate an idea in the writer's own voice, just as one sign of a good writer might be their knack for translating an artist's vision into words.

In this book, we start close to the beginning, taking editorial conversations out of the document, inbox, and office. *Track changes* differs from many handbooks and guides on art writing: rather than tackling formal, grammatical, stylistic, and procedural questions that supposedly can be answered regardless of subject matter, we foreground principles, intentions, desires, and subjects, and then ask how those might influence and inform each part of the editorial process.

To set the stage, we begin with a brief guide to editorial procedures for those newer to the field. This section outlines some of the terms and relationships referred to in the rest of the book, and includes the answers we usually give to the logistical questions that students, young writers, and people shifting into art criticism from another discipline often ask—from what to include in a pitch to what to expect from an editor. We then delve into case studies and reflections.

Our questions about agendas in art criticism assume that critics have some degree of power, a premise explored in several essays in this book, from Annie Godfrey Larmon's "Dirt Is Clean When There Is a Volume" to Leslie Dick's "Soft Talk: Thoughts on Critique" to Merray Gerges's "What's Your Flavor? On Being a Critic of Color in February." This assumption should be distinguished from the presumption that the critic is, as Dick writes, the "*one who knows*": the observer who can conclusively decide whether a work is good or bad.

Rather, we understand that the critic holds power in the sense that they have access to a platform with limited space, so that who they choose to write about, and how, can significantly impact how ideas, opportunities, power, and funding are circulated in the art world. Our stance is implicitly feminist—we take seriously the tasks of expanding who holds the power to tell stories, examining whose stories we tell, and sharing how we tell those stories.

Maintaining a specific perspective or focus in art writing does not only involve what Godfrey Larmon describes as "celebration." Instead, solidarity underlies many agendas as we are defining them here. Solidarity might in fact depend, Godfrey Larmon writes, on some degree of productive friction, or at least the acknowledgment of certain types of disjuncture. Criticism, one mode of creating such friction, is thus central to solidarity.

In several essays, a writer's stated focus on a particular set of practices is a starting point rather than a conclusion—a place to look for questions rather than one to point to as an answer. Emily Watlington begins her text "Writing Through the Lens of Disability Culture" by discussing her intention to center the work of artists with disabilities, which leads to a conversation about navigating the language used by—and the preconceived notions about—that community. In "Correcting Course: Reading a Reframed Canon," Erica Cardwell examines the list of writers on the syllabus she uses to teach a first-year English course, which opens up a set of questions about how to respond to others' expectations for upholding or widening the canon. In "On Bad Art(s Writing)," Kemi Adeyemi considers the complexities of criticism focused on Black artists' work.

Some writers approached our opening questions by sharing a broader manifesto or guide to writing, editing, or publishing; making an agenda involves not only envisioning desired outcomes, but also creating a process to deliver on stated principles. Elisa Wouk Almino's essay "How to Foster a Healthy Writer-Editor Relationship" details her approach to creating and sustaining generous editorial relationships. Likewise, Monica Uszerowicz describes her method of "Pitching with Collaborative Solidarity." In "*Woron* (An Artist's Approach to Writing and Editing): A Manifesto," Kristina Kay Robinson shares how she balances the principles of tradition and innovation across her work. Dessane Lopez Cassell's essay "Word Choice: Who's Your Audience Here?" consists of prompts and questions she often uses to steer writers away from what might be perceived as sophisticated academic language and to encourage more precise articulations.

Another set of texts focuses on the implications of seemingly minor decisions. In "Points of Reference and Belonging," Andy Campbell annotates one of his own reviews to explore the dynamics of drawing comparisons to other artists. Ashley Stull Meyers deliberates on whether to capitalize "Black" in "On Smallness: The Poise and Politics of Capital Letters." In "The Languages of All-Women Exhibitions," Lindsay Preston Zappas gets into the problematic word choices of titles for exhibitions featuring women artists, and suggests how they shape what we expect to see. Ariel Goldberg tests the definition and value of the term "queer art" as it is used in exhibitions and texts through their essay "Simplicity Craving." Yves Jeffcoat discusses the bodily and emotional toll that can come with agreeing to write about work that centers identity in "Write Heavy, Write Slow."

At times, the texts collected here conflict with each other, or offer different understandings of shared concerns; this book does not intend to suggest that there is one single, best way to write or publish that will solve the field's problems. Wendy Vogel's "Neutrality and Feminism" considers how maintaining distance from one's subjects can allow for a more feminist mode of critique; in "On Queer Feminist Critique," Tausif Noor shares why the titular approach might involve posing and following questions more than purporting to offer answers. Amy Fung asks if feminist art writing is possible at all in "How to Review Art as a Feminist and Other Speculative Intents."

Other contributions illuminate how writers have arrived at decisions over time. Yaniya Lee's essay "Art Criticism and the Ethics of Aesthetics: Writing on Richard Mosse's *The Enclave*" is a case study in how mounting a critique of a particular artwork required working through different approaches to form and language. Jillian Steinhauer's "News for Home: Navigating Art Criticism for General Audiences" outlines how her desire to publish art writing that addresses a non-art audience has influenced the way she chooses her subjects and conveys her perspectives. Aruna D'Souza's "Writing in the Reparative Mode" details how her writing practice has shifted in response to wider social changes.

Ultimately, many of these essays explore how we relate to others as writers and editors. Ana Tuazon's "*Real Life* v. *Art Criticism*: A Meta-art Case Study" considers how criticism could benefit from more horizontal and correspondence-based forms, and Jessica Lynne, in "A Letter from an Arts Worker," adopts the epistolary form to outline a set of values for the publication she co-edits. In "Writing in Relation," Re'al Christian advocates for writing that establishes a sense of intimacy, and Dana Kopel explores how editorial work intersects with labor organizing in "For the Comma Pushers."

By gathering all these reflections, we are interested in widening a sense of editorial agency, transparency, and community, while supporting existing commitments to cultivating a richer field of questions and critiques. Our multi-authored approach is a response to one structural problem of the field: mentorship, which we could call a problem of hierarchies, pipelines, stability, and support. Those underrepresented in the field—whether because of class, race, education, or geography—often depend on each other for opportunities and advice on how to move forward, or how to operate from where they are. Given the typical scarcity and privacy of such guidance, how can more writers and editors find real footholds that allow them to step into larger opportunities and more sustainable careers? This publication aims to be a mentor in book form. We incorporate inquiries and conversations that are not otherwise accessible to people starting out or attempting to find traction.

In our effort to collaboratively pursue all those goals, we looked to writers and editors across the US and Canada who have different relationships to the traditional centers of the art world and a range of prior editorial roles. (We would have included many more, if not for the very real constraints of publishing—time, space, funding—and the desire to keep this publication handy and friendly more than authoritative and definitive.) We also opted to use the contributors' biographies as a space to share the many paths people take in, around, and beside art criticism.

TRACKING CHANGES

Writers often look back in order to point forward. We call for change by recalling old histories, detailing untold narratives, and outlining new frameworks. We try to identify when a movement was sparked, or take stock of what happened after an exhibition launched a particular group of artists, or examine how an artist's milieu shaped their work from debut to midcareer survey. In a more mundane sense, editors and writers track changes in Word documents or Google Docs to see what the other party has suggested doing differently and respond to new comments. This practical tool serves as a metaphor for the transparency, action, and communication around small decisions and larger structural changes that we encourage throughout this book.

At the start of this project, I was thinking about the act of critique not only as an editor and critic for a range of publications in New York, but also as a co-organizer—with Katie Giritlian, beck haberstroh, and my generous coeditor Josephine Heston—of a residency program for emerging artists called "rehearsal." We were interested in modes of critique that could embody care and support, and we turned to some of the essays reprinted here for guidance. When I was invited by the curator Janna Dyk to be a curatorial fellow at the feminist nonprofit SOHO20 in 2019, under the umbrella of an initiative called "Rethinking Feminism," I wanted to specify the question: How could we rethink feminism as it undergirds or operates within art publishing? I organized a series of talks with critics and editors who had previously published essays about the stakes of this delicate, assertive, complicated act we call critique. The events were generously funded and hosted by SOHO20 as well as the fellow historic feminist space A.I.R. Gallery.

Those conversations, which thread through this handbook in excerpted form, took place before the pandemic, before the wave of protests against racial violence, before the overturning of *Roe* v. *Wade*—battles with deep histories, stark realities, and long shadows. Through subsequent commissions and edits, we ultimately worked with writers through periods of instability, sickness, and mourning as well as hope and reevaluation. Many people in these pages and in our communities have been working toward unionization at museums and publications, higher and more transparent rates for freelance writers, more diverse staff and contributor lists, and wider conversations on how publishing can drive changes. As part of that chorus, *Track changes* aims to offer companionship and solidarity for those who have long grappled with these questions—and to provide tools for those ready to begin.

A BRIEF PRACTICAL GUIDE TO THE EDITORIAL PROCESS

How do editors assign texts?

How do writers pitch art publications?

What if a writer hasn't published anything before?

What do editors look for in a pitch?

What constitutes an editorial conflict of interest?

How does a writer decide where to pitch?

What's the next step if a writer's pitch is accepted?

What's the next step if a writer's pitch is rejected?

How do writers determine and negotiate their rates?

What are the responsibilities of an editor?

How does someone learn how to edit?

What should an editor do while revising?

How can a writer respond if they disagree with an edit?

A BRIEF PRACTICAL GUIDE TO THE EDITORIAL PROCESS

HOW DO EDITORS ASSIGN TEXTS?

Editors assign texts in a few ways: soliciting pitches and commissioning pieces from regular contributors, reviewing cold pitches from new writers, and extending invitations to other potential contributors. A features editor may reach out to a new writer to ask them to write a specific type of piece based on their prior writing, scholarly or curatorial expertise, and demonstrated interests. This process should involve research and communication. Many of these decisions are subjective and depend on all parties' values and interests as well as the style and other contents of the publication.

HOW DO WRITERS PITCH ART PUBLICATIONS?

In advance of sending a pitch (a brief statement about what a text would argue or explore), both regular contributors and new writers might first check to see if the show, venue, publisher, or artist has been covered recently in the magazine and if the pitch seems appropriate for the publication based on the usual formats and prior coverage. Most magazines prefer to receive a review pitch close to the show's opening, so that the review can be published while the show is still on view for a few weeks. For other types of texts, editors will usually expect the pitch to have a "peg," a current event or forthcoming exhibition that indicates wider interest in the artist or issue at the time of the pitch or anticipated publication date.

A pitch from a new writer will generally contain a brief introduction, a selection of recent or relevant clips of previously published writing, a link to and dates of the exhibition (or other relevant material that explains the "peg" for the piece), and a two- to three-sentence explanation of what the writer wants to argue or focus on in the piece, indicating what kind of text the writer is pitching (review, feature, interview, etc.). For a longer feature, the pitch may be one or two paragraphs. This may vary depending on the editor, format, and publication. Writers should also be transparent in their pitch about any current or prior relationships to, or recent coverage of, the proposed subject, artist, curator, or venue, as editors usually like to be aware of such overlap.

WHAT IF A WRITER HASN'T PUBLISHED ANYTHING BEFORE?

If a writer is new to art criticism and does not have published clips of similar writing, they might share a drafted, unpublished review of a different exhibition (of the same style and length as the text they are pitching) to give the editor a sense of their writing. Another option is to send an academic paper about a similar topic if a writer cannot provide a magazine-style draft. If a writer is pursuing a degree, they might start by contributing to their school's newspaper or magazine, or an undergraduate art publication, as such platforms will be more welcoming of pitches from less established writers. Later those clips can be used while pitching other publications.

Such writers will likely have more success starting with shorter texts and smaller publications, gaining experience with workflows as well as writing and editing techniques before pitching to larger publications. Because larger publications tend to receive a higher volume of pitches, they are less likely to work with someone who does not have prior experience in art criticism or who may not yet be comfortable working with an editor.

Writers may need to conduct more research to find pipelines in these early stages. Common Field, a network of art organizers and organizations, compiled an "Art Publishing List" of national art publications, which may be a good place for emerging writers to identify places to pitch. A writer can also look at the CVs or publication histories of magazine contributors who are a few years ahead in their careers to see where they published their early writing. Another approach is to look at the prior coverage that younger or emerging artists and newer exhibition spaces have received, as those publications may be smaller, more focused, more regional, or more interested in supporting emerging writers, and may be more likely to accept a pitch within their specific purview. The contributor bios in this handbook also indicate how people made forays into art publishing and what forms of support they found helpful along the way.

WHAT DO EDITORS LOOK FOR IN A PITCH?

An editor will use the pitch to gauge how someone thinks and writes, whether their approach to the subject seems informed and considered, and if the intended argument will be feasible to construct within the proposed format. An editor may also consider whether the clips (and pitch) are well written, attentive to the subject at hand, convincingly argued, and grammatically correct. A writer's publication history might indicate how they would approach the subject, or what perspective they might bring to it, and how familiar they are with the context. An editor may request a writer's CV to gauge their familiarity with the topic and check for potential conflicts of interest.

WHAT CONSTITUTES AN EDITORIAL CONFLICT OF INTEREST?

Personal relationships with a subject, and repeated coverage of or employment by the artist or venue, are generally considered conflicts of interest and should be mentioned to an editor in a pitch. An editor would consider whether the writer's ties could unduly limit what they are willing or inclined to discuss, or could lead to a reader's perception of a conflict of interest. This may vary depending on the format of the text and the nature of the relationship.

Other conflicts of interest could emerge depending on the scale and dynamics of the art community in which the writer works. In a smaller city, it is more likely that a writer will personally know an artist or have a prior working relationship with a venue. Such relationships may be less accepted if the writer is working within a larger community.

In some cases, a writer's relationship to or past coverage of an artist or subject, or their ties to and knowledge of a community, may be beneficial. The writer may bring a deeper understanding of the work and its context because of those ties.

HOW DOES A WRITER DECIDE WHERE TO PITCH?

In addition to the above considerations, and without overloading any one editor, a writer may weigh which audiences they want to reach based on what they intend to address in their text. They may consider whether their text will fit within the standard formats of an art publication, or whether a smaller publication with less rigid formats or with a wider range of writing might be a better fit. A medium-specific publication, or one that focuses on artists working with a particular set of concerns, or artists of certain identities, may be a better fit than a more general publication, depending on the artist's prior coverage. A local publication might be more interested in covering a small venue's exhibition of an emerging artist. National publications often need contributors from smaller cities to write about important local shows but may not be able to regularly cover that city given the smaller number of venues there or the limited number of pages for reviews.

A writer may also consider what kind of coverage would most benefit an artist at the present stage of their career, how an artist's practice is usually framed, and whether another perspective might be interesting to flesh out.

WHAT'S THE NEXT STEP IF A WRITER'S PITCH IS ACCEPTED?

The editor will specify a draft deadline and a fee; a writer can ask for confirmation if this information is not provided, and should update the editor if they need to ask for an extension. Many editors prefer to receive drafts as Word documents, though some will accept Google Docs. During revisions, editors and writers should work with tracked changes so that both parties can see what has been suggested and review the proposed edits.

WHAT'S THE NEXT STEP IF A WRITER'S PITCH IS REJECTED?

Generally, it's advised to send a pitch to only one publication at a time, to avoid an issue where the pitch is accepted at multiple publications. However, if a pitch is rejected at a publication, a writer might try pitching it elsewhere, so long as the pitch is still timely and relevant to another publication. As a rough guideline, if a writer has not heard back after one week, they might follow up with the editor. If the writer has never contributed before and/or the writer has not received a response after two weeks, they might pitch the piece elsewhere.

Pitches may be declined for a variety of reasons; depending on an editor's response, a new writer might ask about pitching a different piece later, or they might try working with different publications to find a better fit. Freelance writing often requires contributing to multiple publications because of the low fees at most magazines. If a writer develops a sense of what different publications and editors tend to be interested in, they can direct their pitches accordingly. Editors may prefer to space out contributions from any single writer, depending on their publication's schedule and volume.

HOW DO WRITERS DETERMINE AND NEGOTIATE THEIR RATES?

Many publications have standard fees for pieces of a certain format and length. The rate will generally be discussed during the pitching and commissioning process. Some groups such as Study Hall compile information about rates paid for certain pieces. The Freelance Solidarity Project also has a publicly available database of rates. Editors may be open to writers requesting higher rates, though many publications have firm fees for consistency.

WHAT ARE THE RESPONSIBILITIES OF AN EDITOR?

An editor will often be involved with a text from the commissioning stage through publication. They may consider and incorporate additional suggestions from the copy editor, fact-checker, chief editor, and others along the way. Sometimes they will edit a piece that another editor assigned. More experienced or senior editors will often "top edit," which entails looking over their colleagues' edits to check for overlooked or outstanding issues before the first edit is sent to the writer, or before the text is finalized.

After receiving a draft, an editor may first read through the text to get a sense of its overall condition. Their initial pass will typically focus on developmental edits (considering the larger structure of the text, the flow of ideas, the places where information is introduced, the strength of the arguments and how they could be better supported) and initial line edits (grammatical tweaks, changes to sentence structure, alternative word choices, etc.).

The editor will send the text back to the writer with tracked changes and explanatory comments or prompts for the writer to review. The writer will be expected to respond to the editor's queries, make revisions or accept changes where prompted, and resolve any larger structural issues. These exchanges may happen several times until both parties approve the text. The editor will then typically send the text to a copy editor and review those changes. The editor may then be responsible for preparing the text for publication—choosing which images to use to illustrate the text, uploading the text online, or ensuring that the piece is suitably designed for print.

Beyond editing texts, an editor may be responsible for planning print issues, commissioning sections of a website, identifying potential new writers, and researching upcoming shows and events worth covering.

HOW DOES SOMEONE LEARN HOW TO EDIT?

Editors often learn by doing, but benefit from honing specific skills and finding a mentor. While publications differ in their approach to editing, most expect editors to have a strong grasp of the mechanics of writing as well as familiarity with contemporary art or other primary subjects of the magazine. Reading widely (including but not limited to art criticism) and regularly seeing a range of exhibitions is essential in this regard.

To become familiar with the editing process, aspiring editors might write more and note what kinds of changes their peers or editors make and why. Internships, work with school publications, and entry-level positions at publications can be routes to shadowing and learning from another editor directly. On a more technical level, the *Chicago Manual of Style* is a useful guide that many editors refer to. Purdue Writing Lab also provides useful explanations of common grammatical issues.

WHAT SHOULD AN EDITOR DO WHILE REVISING?

Editors will often begin with larger suggestions (referred to as developmental edits) and later focus on smaller tweaks (line edits). Developmental edits are generally structural and focused on strengthening ideas. An editor may rearrange paragraphs or passages to improve the flow of the text (ensuring a work is described before an interpretation is offered, for example), ask questions about arguments that are hard to follow, and comment on aspects of the text or argument that seem contradictory, potentially problematic, or unresolved. Line edits include fixing typos, rephrasing sentences for clarity, introducing topic sentences and transitions between paragraphs, and implementing standard stylistic and grammatical fixes (for issues such as agreement, dangling modifiers, incorrect use of tenses and punctuation, and overuse of adjectives and adverbs). Especially if the piece has a strict word count, the editor may focus in the later revisions on cutting unnecessary words, combining similar sentences, and specifying vague passages. Across both types of changes, an editor will try to make the text clearer and more concise, and a writer will appreciate some explanatory comments and notes on which parts of the text are most compelling.

HOW CAN A WRITER RESPOND IF THEY DISAGREE WITH AN EDIT?

Editors expect writers to cooperate in responding to edits before any piece is published, but the editorial process is ideally a conversation. Part of the editor's responsibility is to make a text into the best version of itself while persuading a writer that these changes will move the text in that direction. Part of the writer's responsibility is to consider how the editor, as their first and most invested reader, has responded to the text, and to revise the piece to strengthen their ideas and resolve potential issues.

If a writer disagrees with an edit, an editor will usually be open to discussing the change, so long as the writer offers some explanation and provides an alternative way of resolving the issue. For example, a writer may feel that their argument was misinterpreted or misconstrued because of an edit. In this case they might explain (in comment boxes or over email) what they were trying to say and propose a way to make that clearer within the text, perhaps by modifying that passage or revising the surrounding ideas. Or, if an editor suggested an alternate word choice that a writer dislikes, a writer may simply suggest a different option that is closer to what they intended.

If a writer does not understand the reasoning for an edit, an editor should be willing to explain or discuss the change. Writers are generally discouraged from simply ignoring or reverting changes, as the issue the editor flagged will now persist unresolved within the text, which may cause additional issues elsewhere or be flagged by a subsequent editor. Patience and communication are key to this process, as all parties should be invested in ensuring that the text is as clear and well-argued as possible.

PITCHING AND COMMISSIONING

How do editors decide which writer to commission for a text?

How do writers decide which artists and shows to cover?

What are some strategies for disrupting editorial blind spots and gatekeeping?

How can writers and editors advocate for more visibility and criticality for historically underrepresented or misrepresented artists?

LINDSAY PRESTON ZAPPAS: As a writer and as an editor, I'm interested in reframing conversations and not retreading existing histories and narratives. There are moments when we have multiple writers pitching the same idea, and we choose the writer who can provide the more nuanced, interesting perspective that does not reinforce norms. I write and encourage my contributors to write in an inquisitive way, which I feel is more about starting a dialogue among our community of readers, which often consists of artists. My husband, John, and I talk a lot about the idea of punching up instead of down: We can write about a show at the Hammer and be critical and it's going to have less of an effect than if we take down an artist-run show or an artist's first show. But positing the piece toward the community is important. Not having a conclusive statement all the time keeps the texts more open and dialogue-based.

PITCHING WITH COLLABORATIVE SOLIDARITY—TOWARD THE ARTIST, WITH WONDER

MONICA USZEROWICZ

Writing is a solitary practice; writing about art, lonelier still. I might spend days deliberating over the right words, crawling toward what feels right and exploring something that might've been better untouched by my perspective. But I am never truly alone when I write. The writers I love, those worldview-shapers, hover at my shoulder; behind them sits an invisible audience of the artists themselves.

When I'm granted the privilege of choice, the option to pitch what I'd like to cover, I think about collaboration—I engage with work for which I feel deeply and through which I can share ideas that the artist might be able to mine. I build one half of an imagined epistolary dialogue, a humble offering to the artist.

I recently read "Critic in Crisis," an essay by James McAnally for *MARCH*. McAnally advocates for the strategic critic who responds to a need for solidarity and transformation: "Too often, [criticism] harms without repair, or reifies the institution as inevitable. It bludgeons with no trace of solidarity." Writing *to* or for the artist, as if in collaboration, will not resolve these issues, but it removes the critic from a solitary mode of address. Considering the artist—beyond the institutions that may support an artist in service of the institution's own contexts and ideologies, and beyond the true or supposed indispensability of the critic themselves—might situate the text somewhere new, somewhere away from institutions altogether. I write this way by choice, but also by necessity—without an art-historical background, I try to move from a place of care and interest, without perceived authority.

For any writer, access to a publication is valuable—it enables you to work. Clout, though, is a cruel receipt. The problem is not influence or clout itself—that would be reductive—but rather the perpetuation (often by those with some widely acknowledged stature) of gatekeeping, competition, and hierarchical narratives. When a writer has access to such publications, it is therefore imperative to utilize the given space responsibly, with care and respect. Share it. How might one navigate this tension of contributing to a publication that also serves as a gatekeeper throughout the initial process of pitching a story?

1. What will you pitch? With whom do you want to engage in world-building? Whose work provokes even fleeting excitement, a kernel of alacrity that might bloom later, on the page? I am drawn to work that addresses some kind of underbelly or root system, such as the dynamics of local ecosystems or the previously untold histories of a place. I am thinking here of Maren Hassinger's 2019 *Tree of Knowledge* installation at the Boca Raton Museum of Art, which helped tell the story of the Black farming communities that established the surrounding neighborhood, or of the work of the artist—and my friend—Jamilah Sabur, who considers borderlessness by looking to tectonic plates, underwater ridges, the unseen but deep formations of land invisibly connecting so many of us. Some artists' questions focus on the very specific—a language, a single tree, a neighborhood, an ancestral memory—and, in turn, frankly upend my own previously held notions, which at once dissolve or expand. I think of the ecstatic, often collaborative work of Edgar Fabián Frías, who is also a psychotherapist; their installations and performances are inclusive, delightful, and warm, so the participant leaves feeling at least a little bit changed

from how they felt an hour prior. The practice of the artist, filmmaker, and poet Cristine Brache—again, a friend—is visceral; the inherent strangeness and sadness of living feel nearly tangible, even in the archival footage of a short film. Slowly, artists like these crack small parts of the world open; they may challenge long-told anecdotes, presumed authorities, or even the very institution housing the work. This is what I want to support, if only for the selfish reason that it makes me feel excited, intimidated, new. This is how I begin to respond to work, build on it, affirm it.

2. In developing your angle, consider whose stories you believe in and whom you might try to uplift. What if you want to touch the work, to reject the historical, patriarchal positioning of the critic as hierarchically separate from and intellectually superior to the art object? You may be writing a review, but in imagining yourself writing to the artist, perhaps you are expanding on the notions they're exploring—considering the examples given above, maybe you, too, will relearn the history of a place, a language, a figure. Your previous understandings, your sense of self, the emotive qualities of the work and their impact, the potentiality of all these forces and beliefs become unexpected angles and places of research. Imagine the artist reading it: what do you want *them* to see, to learn themselves?
3. Ask yourself: Is this a story you can—or should—tell? Consider the capitalistic illusion of unlimited capacity projected onto all cultural producers. As one of few arts writers in a "small" city, I feel the pressure to help showcase as many local artists as I can, as often as I can, while maintaining critical distance. As a person with chronic physical pain, I've developed more compassion for my limitations. Write what you can tend to with

care. Also consider your own voice. You will never share the lived experience of the artist; remain mindful of the space you're taking up and the lenses through which you approach their work. Can you interview the artist before you write? Can you explore together? If you can't, how might you write with a sense of sympathetic consciousness toward their work, their view? If the artist is no longer living, what would you like to have said to them? Critique or praise is naturally transformed when it comes from a place of interest, of attention, of at least attempted understanding. How has the work moved you? Challenged you? Maybe you write about this in a way that's personal. Maybe you simply write from that place of attunement.

4. You can maintain a sense of distance in your pitch with the understanding that your identities and relations will inevitably inform what you're writing. If you have some relationship to the artist, some emotional investment, acknowledging that is important; it will help an editor decide if your position is the one they are seeking, and later, it may help an editor probe your blind spots. It may also indicate your ability to translate and measure the artist's intentions—sometimes the emotional investment that accompanies an existing relationship can inhibit the writing, while in other instances, it might facilitate it. This is exciting.
5. Within your pitch, you don't have to decode or elucidate the work for the editor. You can state your desire to explore, query, and investigate the work through the act of writing. (This might be easier to do once you have established a relationship with an editor, who can then trust you to explore with rigor.) Maintain your curiosity.
6. Relish the moments when your conversations build on the work, when it feels like your perspectives have broadened from your dialogue. In 2021, I interviewed

the multidisciplinary artist Natalia Lassalle-Morillo about *Retiro*, a hybrid film-performance project she created collaboratively with her mother, Gloria Morillo Cabán. Lassalle-Morillo is from Puerto Rico, the place of my own mother's birth; in discussing the project, the artist taught me about my ancestry and, in turn, recognized and defined inspirations for the work she hadn't yet located—though they were always there, always with her. The generosity of sharing can extend the contours of an idea. Like a spiral, I read her, she read me; the imprint of what we learned now exists, unwittingly, in a web of relations.

LESLIE DICK: Annie, at one point in your essay "Dirt Is Clean When There Is a Volume," you say, "Art criticism is the art of wielding power." But what power does the art critic really have? The market dictates so much.

ANNIE GODFREY LARMON: Of course the role of the critic has changed very much over the past sixty, seventy years. But I'm often thinking about materialism and power in terms of the artists that I choose to write about. Often, they don't have access to the same power or capital as other artists who are regularly written about, or who fit into a certain subject position that happens to have more readily accessible education or funds or resources. So when I talk about criticism as an act of wielding power, I mean that it involves sharing—or lending—by virtue of including an artist in the limited real estate, especially of a print magazine. It involves saying that, for its successes or its failures, this is worthy of attention, and of course it has a signaling function for the market, for galleries, for opportunities.

LD: Absolutely.

AGL: I mean, I was publishing with *Artforum* for six years and God knows if anyone ever even read my reviews. So often these things fall into a vacuum. Nevertheless, I think the more material that we can generate about artists we find worthy of attention and the more discourses, the more conversations, horizons, we can open up to that work, the more power we're able to share with the objects of art criticism. So that's where that point was coming from—I certainly don't believe in the inflated role of the critic these days.

LD: It was interesting to me because in "Soft Talk" I was trying to articulate what a nonhierarchical discourse would be, which isn't to say that it isn't powerful. It is powerful—in the discovery of and possibility for complexity that can come through the process of engaging an artwork—but the power is a little more distributed, decentralized. Although I write about art quite frequently, I'm not in the world of writing short-form pieces, I'm not trying to create a connection between a whole bunch of people who would read *Artforum* all over the world and a show that happened in Brooklyn in a small gallery that maybe only a few people go to. And it's funny because the people I write about, have written about, are people like Eva Hesse, Louise Bourgeois, Hannah Wilke, Marisa Merz. These are people I can't wield any cultural capital with—you know, Louise Bourgeois is Louise Bourgeois. I can say anything about her, and it's not going to shift her stature. So there emerges a very interesting question: Do your politics and your commitment to solidarity as a feminist take the form of finding under-recognized women-identifying artists and then writing about them, on principle? I'm intrigued by what kind of principles people have, about who they write about and why and what. I don't really have any principles. My attitude is: if I get excited about it, usually I can't understand what's going on, so the only way I can understand the process of what's happening in the show and in this artwork is by writing it through, thinking it through, engaging with it—only that process of writing will take me to a place where I feel less confused and conflicted about it, or give me a chance to interpret and translate my own excitement into a more concrete form.

WHAT'S YOUR FLAVOR? ON BEING A CRITIC OF COLOR IN FEBRUARY

MERRAY GERGES

Many years ago, I saw Richard Hill speak on a panel titled "Art Criticism and the Ecology of Art." There, he pointed to his position as one of a handful of Indigenous scholar-critic-curators in Canada, and—if memory serves me correctly—how that weighed on the kind of criticism he could level at work produced by members of his community, which had just recently begun to achieve visibility and acknowledgment by the settler-Canadian art world.

Hill's comment, for me, conjured up a clip from *Mean Girls* (2004), where main characters Regina George, the high-school "queen bee," and Cady Heron, the "new girl from Africa," gossip until the outfit of a passerby, a woman of vague non-white origin, catches Regina's eye. "Oh my god! I love your skirt—where did you get it?" she gushes. But as soon as this woman leaves the scene, Regina turns back to Cady and whispers, "That is the ugliest effing skirt I've ever seen."

Though this analogy doesn't 100 percent mirror Hill's dilemma, I've asked myself many related questions since I saw him speak in 2013: Are critics who are people of color (POC) expected to be representatives of the marginalized communities that they belong to—and if so, how does that inform whether they sugarcoat or critique bluntly? Does the Bambi/Thumper rule—"If you can't say something nice, don't say nothing at all"—especially hold water in marginalized communities? If the role of the critic is to survey, demystify, and contextualize art for an informed audience, then is the critic of color tasked with elucidating identity politics, to be a mouthpiece or a mediator to predominantly white, uninformed audiences? To cheerlead and advocate for the artists of color whose work might be considered too esoteric, or too "special interest," by these audiences? When there are so few POC artists and even fewer POC critics, is the onus on critics in my position to champion them because, seemingly, no one else will? What actually, tangibly results from roundups of diversity?[1] What happens after we've shaken our heads and glanced at stats that testify that the landscape is bleaker than we'd thought, that maybe we aren't as "inclusive" as we'd lauded ourselves to be?

I am a woman of color who passes: visible enough to be subject to the question "Where are you *really* from?" but usually able to avert it with, "I'm a Canadian citizen." So when I was asked by the editors at *Canadian Art* to weigh the virtues and the perils of an initiative like Black History Month—or African Heritage Month, as it is called where I live in Nova Scotia—I wondered: How much space can I take up without detracting from those who've been systemically dispossessed of it?

If I'm given an opportunity because I might be one of the few writers of color on an editor's contact list, and if I'm selected for positions elsewhere—where the first thing I'm told is, "You're *very lucky* you got this. It was very competitive"—because I say I'm interested in writing about tokenism, and it's hot to purport to support marginalized voices, then where does that leave me when I don't feel like speaking to any of this? I can't help but wonder if I'm approached on the basis of fulfilling some undisclosed diversity quota, to be paranoid of institutional claims of meritocracy and, therefore, of my own merit.

Where is this tension coming from? Is it self-imposed or is it internalized? Take into consideration my lived experience: In the 10 years I have lived in Canada, it wasn't until strangers on the street approached me to point out that I look like Ilana from *Broad City* that I encountered someone who resembled me on a screen. I was known in my suburban southwestern Ontario high school as "the girl from Egypt" / "Cleo" / "Fez" (the exchange student in *That 70s Show*), invited to sit at lunch with my white peers only to be quizzed about what it was like to live in the pyramids and how I learnt to speak more fluent English than them if I had only just gotten here (ignoring, of course, the necessity for the colonized to speak the colonizer's language better than them), and then getting dragged by the hand to be introduced to the only two other Arabic speakers at our school.

All these years later, how could I not feel responsibility tugging at me when the first thing that I notice when I enter most art spaces in Nova Scotia is that I'm the only person of color—and it *cuts*—and I see individuals and institutions relentlessly performing ally theatre with lip-service proclamations of support?

When I moved back to Halifax for a residency in October 2015, the first POC I encountered in the three weeks after I arrived advised me that I ought to consider my writing practice as what they called a "creek of [my] privilege"—to lend a voice and give space to those rarely afforded either. I revisit many of the questions I asked myself earlier when I remember that I am in a place that is home to one of the first and largest settlements of black people in Canada, where Africville was razed just under 60 years ago[2] to make room for urban development, a place where incidences of anti-blackness still abound.[3]

The very fact that people still ask whether we need Black History Month is symptomatic of the belief in a so-called "post-racial" society. This debate arises annually, roughly taking the same shape: one side denigrates the relegation and the pigeonholing and pushes for integration, the other side asks what we would be left with, whether we'd talk about it at all in the absence of a designated month.

And while Black History Month programming, at its best, can be an exposure opportunity for emerging black artists, the visibility comes at a price in this essentialist context.

"You're given your month, but [you're treated like] this is not real art. There's no real level of engagement with the work," said Pamela Edmonds, a Toronto-based curator, when I interviewed her in 2014 about her involvement with the Black Artists Network of Nova Scotia and the countless exhibits she's curated that address the politics of representation.

Mind you, it's totally fair for the editors who commissioned this article to anticipate that I would take up this proposal. Last May, I wrote about being only one of a handful of POC at a large-scale art-criticism conference,[4] and one of the writing samples I've submitted to all the mentorships and internships I've applied to in the two years since graduating is titled "Insufficient Funds: A Case Study of Veiled Tokenism."

I had the option to decline this writing opportunity. I deliberated on forwarding it to a black Canadian writer. But, as Jessica Lynne, co-founder of *ARTS.BLACK*, an art-criticism journal from black perspectives, has said, "Black writers shouldn't be called upon only to write about 'Black' things."[5]

Those same editors told me I would be welcome to pitch any other time on other topics. Though the door wasn't exactly closed in my face, I still have reservations about the instances I'm invited in.

Ultimately, I took this opportunity to open the dialogue about diversity in Canadian art publishing, to encourage editors and curators to diversify their rosters of writers, to push those gatekeepers to reach out to writers of color not just when their "flavor of the month" is propelling the rotation of think pieces and listicles.

I must remember that I have agency in my self-representation, too.

"If you're presenting yourself as the other all the time, then you're doing it to yourself. The institution will do it to you, no problem whatsoever. I think you know when you're being put in that position," Edmonds told me. "It's about being more strategic, if you're a cultural worker, to not allow that to happen. Those systems are set up to tokenize you. They're not always aware of their own self to be able to not do it. There's no excuse anymore; I'm not letting them get away with it."

Me neither.

This article first appeared as Merray Gerges, "What's Your Flavour? On Being a Critic of Colour in February," *Canadian Art*, February 18, 2016, https://canadianart.ca/essays/on-being-a-critic-of-colour-in-february/.

1 Alison Cooley, Amy Luo, and Caoimhe Morgan-Feir, "Canada's Galleries Fall Short: The Not-So Great White North," *Canadian Art*, 2015.

2 Africville Heritage Trust, "The Story," https://africvillemuseum.org/africville-heritage-trust/the-story/.

3 Lezlie Lowe, "Halifax's Hidden Racism," *The Coast*, 2009.

4 Merray Gerges, "Who Gets to Be a Critic?," *Walker Reader*, 2015.

5 An Paenhuysen, "Where Are All the Young Black Art Critics?," *Contemporary And*, 2016.

MIRA DAYAL: Merray, in your essay "On Being a Critic of Colour in February," you write, "If the role of the critic is to survey, demystify, and contextualize art for an informed audience, then is the critic of color tasked with elucidating identity politics for predominantly white, uninformed audiences?" And "Is the onus on critics in my position to champion them because, seemingly, no one else will?" That essay was published in 2016. How do you feel your role as a critic has changed since then? In your bios, you often say that you write "around art." That phrase suggests that you're trying to shape the contours of the discussion rather than insert yourself directly into it.

MERRAY GERGES: I wrote this essay for *Canadian Art* a couple of months before I started working there. A white editor got in touch with me in February and said, you know, you've written about tokenism in the art world before—do you want to write this piece about Black History Month for us? I thought, that's funny—I must be the only person of color on your contacts list. So I wrote this piece totally calling out the imperative to only ask a writer of color to participate in a conversation when their month comes around. And at the same time, I remember negotiating with myself and thinking, Should I hand this over to a Black critic? And then I thought, no, then I would be perpetuating the exact same thing that happened to me, and I actually have relative privilege in this context, where I can call this out and not get in very much trouble, because I'm in Canada. This piece went viral, because I said some things that seemed really obvious to me but that hadn't been addressed.

When I was hired as an editorial fellow that summer, there seemed to be a sometimes spoken, sometimes unspoken expectation that my writing, my output, my presence in this institution would single-handedly undo forty years of exclusion. This was the summer of 2016, and the climate was one of urgency, with this attitude that *we need to do something about this and you need to be the one to do it because we don't know how*. At first, I gave in to that pressure, partly because I didn't know how to resist it, but also because I benefited from it. I made a name for myself as the writer doing this work that the publication had never done before. But I started to feel that writers of color were expected to have certain conversations. I wrote this essay before I had experienced any of this, actually, and then I came to experience it firsthand. I resent being cornered into being the cheerleader. What if I see a show by an artist of color and I think it's bad? I should be able to say that

I think it's bad. Who does it serve, really, if the conversation doesn't go that way? White critics aren't going to say that it's bad.

This became so clear to me when I went to the 10th Berlin Biennale. As most of you know, it was an unprecedentedly diverse biennale—two-thirds of the artists were artists of color and over half of those were Black—and people were talking about it as an "identity politics" or "Black" biennale. I noticed that so much of the press on it was very congratulatory, but then I found myself having conversations with white critics who would say, "Actually, I thought it was bad," or, "I didn't get it," even though that wasn't how they were writing about it. That affirmed the position I felt I was in: Mainstream critics are not writing critically about this work, so by implication, we're the only ones who not only *could* but *should*.

JESSICA LYNNE: Yeah, that tension is so strange. I do feel a responsibility—and a happy obligation—to write about Black artists, specifically Black women artists …

MG: But we shouldn't be the only ones.

JL: Right—let's say you'd never seen an artist's work before. You shouldn't be called to write about their work just because they're Black and you're Black. I've benefited, in New York specifically, from a certain type of visibility as a Black art critic. *ARTS.BLACK* began with this question: *Where are all the young Black art critics?* But what is the next set of questions? I should be able to say that I love Black women artists *and* that they don't get written about in ways that are sufficient, or critical, or rigorous. But there are multiple other questions that we could ask, and multiple solutions.

MD: How have you handled that dynamic with your writers? To what degree do you encourage criticality? Do you expect writers to see a variety of shows and then maintain a balance of who they're writing about and how they're writing about them?

JL: A lot of people will pitch to us and say that they are so thankful for this space for Black art and Black artists—which is true, that is what our space is for, and it's also a sign of what's not out there—but it's also okay to say that you didn't love a show. You don't have to write about the show. We/I try to be really direct about that. If you commit to this work or obligation—in my case, writing about Black women—there's something that the essayist Rachel Kaadzi Ghansah said that I'll paraphrase: I'm really only interested in writing about artists and cultural producers I care about, and I want to write about them in ways that have not already been written. She's interested in the durationality of things. That, too, is a possible solution to this problem. With some Black artists, the same line, the same rhetoric, comes up over and over again. For that reason, I think it still matters that artists and writers of color try to be committed to each other, but the task of creating new language around a body of work also matters. There are inspiring, exciting, and experimental ways to fulfill that obligation to write about artists who are "like you."

WRITE HEAVY, WRITE SLOW
YVES JEFFCOAT

I choose to write about race and identity in art. I choose to continually aggravate and then suture the wound. When I write about art, I must go through it. I must swallow it. It cannot remain on the tip of the tongue. And because I often accept commissions for texts on Black artists and about Black life, I am inevitably drawn into it. I end up lingering on pain, feeding my anger, detaching from empathy, and questioning the validity of my feelings. I am compelled to anatomize my being.

Cultural workers who are invested in "making revolution irresistible," as Toni Cade Bambara put it, often talk about the importance of uplifting marginalized voices and work as a means to challenge the status quo and transform society. And those of us who are part of oppressed groups justifiably reiterate how necessary it is to preserve our histories, share our stories, and tell our truths. We endure because we believe our work has purpose. But the urgency of the message does not nullify the difficulty of carrying and delivering it. I think of writer Lorraine Hansberry's rumination: "Do I remain a revolutionary? Intellectually—without a doubt. But am I prepared to give my body to the struggle or even my comforts? This is what I puzzle about." The implication was that Hansberry—who died of pancreatic cancer at age thirty-four—had not already given her body to the struggle. Beyond the fact that merely existing in a marginalized body puts one at risk, the reality is that repeatedly writing about our race and identities takes a toll on our mental and physical states.

This is the trade-off in intentionally writing pieces that center our identities. We may be driven to write them, fueled by our values and mission. But we must also understand that in doing so, we may subject ourselves to exhaustion, existential questioning, guilt, traumatization, overload, and other problems that can harm us or distort our sense of self.

For many valid reasons, we may rush to pitch or accept an assignment: We need the money; we'd like the byline; we want the experience; we have something to say. But in the pause before a decision, we have the agency and the time to determine if and why our answer is "yes" or "no," and we owe no one an explanation. In slowing down, we can ask ourselves whether we are eager *and* ready to write a piece, without weighing, say, payment and potential exposure more heavily than emotional cost. Rather than pursuing assignments based on what and how much we think we should be writing, we can take stock of our emotional availability to determine what we are capable of writing well in a specific moment. After all, we are the ones who must weather the writing process and its aftermath.

Analyzing and critiquing art that encourages thoughtful engagement also requires us to immerse ourselves in the history, context, and space of that art. We might have to visit galleries, thumb through catalogs and textbooks, interview artists, watch videos, and attend lectures. Through our research, we could be transported to previous eras, distant cities, and unfamiliar cultures—in person and in our imaginations. This task can be particularly burdensome when the art is loaded with contentious subject matter, sensitive historical themes, or potentially distressing imagery and references—especially when our personal experiences exacerbate our emotional response. To write about art, we have to sit with our own and other people's narratives, baggage, mistakes, and accomplishments. This is no small task, since simply viewing art can elicit intense feelings. We must acknowledge that the content that consumes us when we're absorbed in the scrutiny of artwork is often taxing, and it inhabits our minds for an extended period.

During the research and writing processes, it helps to balance isolation and interaction in a way that feels healthy. When we are feeling stuck or overwhelmed, pushing through is not the only option. Take breaks from the work, and use all the time you are allotted (or ask for more). Consult with other writers, or speak with friends who have consented to letting you vent to them. Consider incorporating your experience into your writing. Then write.

When the raw emotion has settled, I may turn to practices that force me to step away from intellectual reasoning and refocus on visceral experience. I may shift my attention to the reasons why I persist in writing, so as not to become mired in the quicksand of trauma and cynicism. Sometimes, I practice breathing exercises. Other times, I've found it useful to compose a mantra and meditate on it. The silent repetition provides a simple way to wrangle spiraling thoughts and calm anxiety. I've also made time to walk or drive aimlessly, removing the demands of purpose and productivity. In reconnecting with my body and with the present moment, I'm able to manage dissociation and stress with little exertion. But no matter what method you choose, know that there is no guilt or shame in refusing to let the work chew you up and spit you out.

The process will still be difficult—we will still be challenged to be vulnerable, critical, and honest on paper while reckoning with our own reactions to the subject matter. And while receiving edits and revising our work can compound any emotions that writing may have surfaced, it's beneficial to remember that editing is a conversation, and that having the opportunity to craft nuanced arguments will allow us to have more confidence in the impact and legacy of our work. It's easy to become overwhelmed when revisiting heavy work. It's also easy to be defensive about suggested changes when a topic is charged or hits home and was exhausting to write about. But ultimately, it's advantageous to stay open-minded and pragmatic with edits to avoid undue stress.

An editor and writer are guaranteed not to have the same lived experiences and perspectives, and establishing trust with a new editor can be tough. This is especially true when the editor wields relative power or privilege through their social identities, and the collaborative text is criticism or opinion. It's reassuring when editors are truthful about sentiments that they don't understand and when they ask questions rather than make assumptions. Then I can worry less about an editor's intentions and have more confidence in their allyship in delivering a clear and potent text. I may be accustomed and willing to dissect themes related to my identities, but I am also often anxious about the quality and reception of my writing. Sincere affirmation that acknowledges the weight or value of the work can help to assure writers that we are being supported and not used. It reminds us that we're not just enduring labor for the sake of optics.

We care for ourselves when we finish a piece and move on, letting go of the side effects of writing it rather than letting them fester. This does not mean that we disengage with the subjects and ideas that we find meaningful. Nor does it change the fact that we may be tired and overburdened by the pressure to put ourselves under a microscope and prove our worthiness as critics. It does allow us to consciously reject burnout and return to our core reasons for writing, so that we may begin anew when we're ready to write again.

AMY FUNG: There was a certain time when being gay was bad for your career. Do you think that still exists now? Or being a feminist? Is that bad for your career?

ARIEL GOLDBERG: No, I think it's really good. And it's really new that it's really good.

AF: Well, isn't it sort of perpetuating the same problem, but on the flip side? Like, how can a queer writer or a feminist writer speak outside of that group?

AG: It's not a feasible construct. It doesn't feel real. All playing to the brands and the marketing.

AF: Yes, but I guess in the small, niche world of art criticism, there's not that much diversity, right? So to be known as the queer writer in this city's art scene ... there's a danger to that, too, or to assigning women writers to write about women's art. Like, why aren't the men writing about this?

LINDSAY PRESTON ZAPPAS: But do you feel that the writer's identity is crucial to understanding what they're writing about? Or the idea of showing your cards as a writer?

AF: It depends on what work they've done.

Anyone can write meaningfully about anything if they care, if they engage. But editors want to play it safe. I see that happening over and over again, and I think it's dangerous. I want to hear from the other editors as well …

LPZ: There are certain writers (white, male) that my editors and I know are going to write about a certain genre of art in the same, predictable way. And, often we decide that there might be a more interesting writer who could comment on that and bring some nuance to it and make it far more interesting.

AF: But then what about the opposite, like assigning that guy to cover a show of a Black artist?

LPZ: We've had that happen too. It takes the right type of writer. We just had a white male writer write about "Soul of a Nation" at the Broad Museum, which is a history of Black art in America. I do feel like he had to work for it because although he sees that work and had written about much of it before, he had to climb up the mountain a little more to do the work for that show.

MIRA DAYAL: And in some ways, it's good to force writers to do that work. If they hadn't reviewed that show, they might not have put in that work, and I'm sure that will inform what they do in the future, even if not in explicit ways. Having a supposed mismatch of identities of artist and writer can be beneficial.

AF: I want to see more of it. But a lot of editors I've talked to are wary of doing that, because it's too much of a risk on their part.

AG: It's also about who the editors are, what their vocabularies are, and how competently they can guide the text when the supposed identities of the reviewer are not stemming from the lived experiences or conditions of the artist. I remember when Peter Schjeldahl's review of the Whitney Biennial came out, it was like, how did this happen in the *New Yorker*? Where were the editors? Why do certain people still have columns? Why are certain people still staff writers? All those people who write things ignorantly and still have a platform, and even editors who can't catch certain things and challenge them—I want them to fall. I want them to retire.

AF: But when they retire, those columns will retire with them, right?

AG: They'll just have a bunch of freelancers take their place.

WRITING

CRITIQUE AND POSITIONS

What is at stake when writing with a critical versus a celebratory lens?

How does authority factor into the act of critique?

Can critique be a form of care?

How does emphasizing one's subjectivity relate to delivering honest criticism?

ON BAD ART(S WRITING)

KEMI ADEYEMI

When writing on black artists, we often have an agenda: Demonstrate an anti-racist critical discourse in which the artist's depth and complexity is fully illuminated. We are often writing in the wake of white writers who misread, misinterpret, or altogether ignore black artists; writers who perpetuate false binaries between high and low art, art and popular culture, and art and activism; and writers who don't take basic steps to research the histories, techniques, and vocabularies with which black artists are working. Such art criticism often says more about the enduring ignorance and laziness of white supremacist discourse than it does about the formal and conceptual concerns of black artists. The stakes of writing about black artists can feel especially high in these conditions. We often write from a defensive position, worrying that critique might give people more tools with which to misread and/or denigrate black artists. Critics working from a place of white fragility can be afraid to generate critiques for fear of looking like they don't know what they're talking about or of appearing to be racist. The pressure can be intensified when we are writing in small and midsize cities, and when we are circulating in tight-knit arts communities: We fear our writing will be taken as a personal attack and/or will have direct consequences on artists' capacities to fund, create, and exhibit their work.

Our commitments to developing rich, critically informed writing on black artists can come up against an interesting burden, though: chronic positivity. When black artists—and minoritarian artists, more broadly—do not receive critical writing that engages the formal and conceptual intricacies of their work, and points out what could make the work stronger, they are susceptible to constant praise that can become tokenizing. That constant praise often comes from seemingly progressive, radical, anti-racist, decolonial, feminist, etc. circles that are paradoxically too invested in the progress narratives, respectability politics, and/or celebrity cultures of the capitalist art market to provide real dissent. Art criticism that refuses to critique contributes to a negative feedback loop in which artists and the discourse around them stagnates.

There are, of course, many reasons we may want to critique black work, and these reasons are not exclusive of black art and artists. Sometimes the work could be sharper in its formal execution. We might have concerns about the conceptual genealogies or aims of the work. We might be tasked with writing about an artist who is a known abuser, or has what we feel are "bad" politics, or performs a marketable blackness that we feel capitulates to the art market's voracious appetite for easily consumable difference. The challenge is how to richly detail artists' aesthetic concerns while skillfully and strategically drawing out historical and contextual information to make an informed critique. Such strategizing can only happen after we have plotted our own relationships to (the politics of) blackness, and after we have acknowledged and attended to the expectations we have of black art and artists.

Great arts writing subsequently depends on a belief that race has an effect on the production and circulation of art. Great arts writing is responsively fleshed out through carefully conducted research, and is necessarily self-reflexive. It also depends on and thrives among people and institutions who believe that critique is a form of care, to use Mandy Harris Williams's language: "Earnest social and cultural critique is, and always will be, the desire to get to the bottom of the thing for the liberation of truth and therefore, all people involved." Critique is a method of holding one another to the highest standard, and the material labor of arts writing "forms necessary data for the efforts at redesigning society towards more caring and liberated ends." Put another way, arts writing can and should be an effort to wield critical thought in the service of a more just society. Practicing critique as a form of care disabuses us of the belief in objectivity that still plagues arts discourse, and honors moments when we want more: from a work, from an artist, from a community, from an institution. Let's orient to these moments not as a lack but as pressure points of vulnerability that produce (our) desire(s). In doing so, we implicate ourselves as writers in ways that might generate more ethical, holistic systems in which the work of black artists is engaged in all their complexity.

ARIEL GOLDBERG: I have not received a lot of criticism for my book. I think that's because I was self-reflecting, really thinking about how I'd been complicit in all of these systems and how I continue to be, how I benefit from all the attention I've gotten from the book. This year, I received a real critique of how I framed my Jewish heritage in the book, from somebody who is an academic and studies Orientalism. That was really amazing. I can count on one hand the number of times people have given me really useful feedback that then informs how I move forward. I want more of that. I think there's a real taboo around that in criticism.

MIRA DAYAL: You were speaking to me earlier about everyday activities and decisions that accompany the writing of art criticism—choices in terms of shows you go to see or the other writing you do in tandem with these larger writing projects—and how they affect your criticism.

AG: I think there's only so much that writing can do. You are limited by the language, form, and publication. Alongside the writing that I chose to do, I also wanted to organize events. One of the greatest things that happened to me while drafting this book and distributing it as a self-published pamphlet is that the director of the Poetry Project at the time, Stacy Szymaszek, said, why don't we work together—you can be a curator here. I was putting the theories into practice by choosing who to curate and deciding how to introduce their practices. I did that for four years, four of the seven years that I spent writing the book. Putting the theory into practice is really important. Being on the side of the thing you're critiquing, actually doing it and failing at it, is tremendously useful.

DIRT IS CLEAN WHEN THERE IS A VOLUME
ANNIE GODFREY LARMON

In the spring of 2015, as an editor at *Artforum*, I commissioned a short text from Jo Baer on the occasion of Agnes Martin's traveling retrospective. Because the women's names are often said in the same breath in the context of Minimalism—they were the only two women, out of twenty-eight artists, in Lawrence Alloway's landmark 1966 "Systemic Painting" exhibition at the Guggenheim—I proposed that Baer share a personal anecdote, or write about a work that interested her, or discuss the ways in which her work was in dialogue with Martin's. Baer sent the following response:

> I'm afraid I have nothing to contribute vis-à-vis Agnes Martin and her work. I met her only once, in the early 1960s (at an opening at the Robert Elkon Gallery in New York for the first show by my then husband, John Wesley), and she was pretty strange, bitching to him about her lack of prestige compared with Robert Rauschenberg et al. Her work (like Robert Ryman's) has never interested me: The lyrical is not my meat. Sorry, I know our "well-known" women's voices should show solidarity, but even in death?

We decided to run her reply—a sharp barb in the midst of near-hagiography. The sentiment offered a critical corrective to the essentializing narrative that aligns these artists because of two factors: their gender and their engagement with geometric abstraction. Baer's note has returned to me time and again, for the words *should* and *solidarity*, for the idea that the conditions of these terms might change posthumously, and for the attendant apology.

We can only speculate whether Baer might have responded more generously, or not at all, should Martin still be living. Yet the fact that she found the distinction worthy of remark and that she emphasized her sense of obligation suggests she might have been more circumspect in her reply. There is, of course, a difference between not responding and stating a refusal to respond. And this refusal wasn't simply that; it includes a stinging anecdote laced between statements of disinterest. Despite its important objective, an aspect of Baer's response irked me—not its bristle, but its underlying conflation of notions of solidarity and celebration. Though the latter may well be part of the former, solidarity is only handicapped by the idea that it must be celebratory.

What constitutes a gesture of solidarity in the context of critical production is a complicated equation, not least because the conditions that shape agency, representation, and lack are always shifting. For women artists who worked in the postwar period—with marginal representation in institutions and the market, and with support networks that were not as robust as those shared by women today—solidarity might have meant championing work based on a confluence of gender and merit. It might have meant sharing the spotlight. But if we take solidarity at its definition, as unity among people who have the same interests and standards, we must retool the term. To uphold those shared interests and standards, we must consider solidarity beyond inclusion to embrace rigorous critique and the formation of communities dedicated to both mentorship and productive antagonism—perhaps, mentorship by way of productive antagonism.

In the dealings of women, is it not greater to leverage the stirrings of contradiction, rift, and dissensus, and to come together in discourse *because* of these stirrings, than to quiet them in the service of "solidarity"? Baer's statement—in contradistinction to its cattiness, but because of its dissent—is a feminist gesture. Though its assumptions about solidarity may be outmoded, the sentiment's actual, functional expression, insofar as it complicates such categorical approaches to history, is indeed one of solidarity, more rigorously conceived.

To set the stage for a discussion of criticism and mentorship among women in the contemporary art world, it seems important to acknowledge a weirdness or discomfort—corroborated only empirically and anecdotally—that attends blunt address of the practical and identifiable ways in which women participate and are compensated differently in its institutions, marketplaces, and spaces of visibility. My proximity to these topics blurs their edges, but I can only attest to the complicated feelings they summon, to the almost prickly response such topics trigger in my colleagues and friends who identify as women. I speak of feelings because feelings, too often considered gendered, are similarly dismissed in such discussions, as vital as they may be to the way power is manifested. Indeed, although art is a place where, as the artist Hannah Black recently described, "we can treat the self as historical and social material,"[1] there remains a shared unease with the category of woman writer, woman artist, woman curator or art historian. This is not only because both the criteria and relevance of the category are unclear, but because to identify with the category—as is the case with any such identification—is inherently to exclude oneself from others. This kind of identification brings with it the risk of accepting that women are the bearer of gender, a construction from which male-identified subjects might be exempt.

But moreover, why do female categories seem always already diminutive, even embarrassing, especially for those who ostensibly belong to them? Can it be chalked up to internalized misogyny? Or does it have more to do with a hesitation surrounding the blunt political sociology of gender in the art world, or the regressive formations of gender and representation that risk generalization and stereotyping? Perhaps it is an allergy to the ways in which categories of identity are easily packaged and exploited by the market. Or it could come from the shade of defeat these categories stir up—by rejecting such categories, one distances oneself from the marginalization they suggest.

It may also be a by-product of the sense that cultural discourse already dealt with these problems in the 80s and 90s and we should be on to less obvious and more nuanced questions of identity. The embrace of intersectional theory—an identity politics in which one's sense of self is informed by experiences based on encounters of class, gender, race, and sexuality—makes it difficult to return to such reductive terms. We may write from an intersectional perspective about intersectional work, but this doesn't diminish the necessity to point to the very material discrepancies between the problematic but deeply lived categorical positions of, specifically, men and women.

This is to say that there is a disparity between theory and practice. Though we long ago metabolized the concept that there were and are many feminisms, that various discriminations are always imbricated in our experiences of sexism and racism, and that identity is reified by institutional power, there remains an enormous economic and professional inequity between genders. This is well trodden but perennially important ground. In 2014, the *New York Times* ran an article that revealed women "run just a quarter of the biggest art museums in the United States and Canada, and they earn about a third less than their male counterparts." And in 2015, Amelia Jones reminded us in her essay "On Sexism in the Art World" that "works by women artists are still worth far less than similar works by men from the same generation and locale." Last year, the *Times* published "Female Artists Are (Finally) Getting Their Turn," a piece about the spate of exhibitions that opened this past spring [2016] featuring women-themed surveys, which Barbara Kruger describes as "playing catch-up after centuries of women's marginality and invisibility." (This outward institutional acknowledgment of discrimination is a start, but one that seems exceedingly belated.) This is all further complicated by the fact that in the system's pipeline, over 60 percent of students in MFA programs are women.[2]

It's an exhausting topic to rehash. This unease might be located in a contradiction fundamental to the problem: the contemporary art world is a cultural field that not only prides itself, but also generates content and capital based on inclusion, difference, and pluralism. But this is only flimsily manifested in both institutions and social networks. As Suhail Malik has written, "It may be that despite their sincerely wrought advances, the theoretical-political demands of contemporary art's critical understanding serve to offset and exculpate the generally abysmal gender inequality in position, wealth, and what might be called exhibition-power in contemporary art."[3] It's hard to imagine this contradiction—the sense that we have culturally and theoretically transcended misogyny in the face of material evidence otherwise—wouldn't incur some form of psychological disenfranchisement.

In spite, or perhaps *because*, of women's convoluted relationship to power and the shifting contours of solidarity, there remains a sense that there is a gulf separating rivalry and partiality between women. This binary may well simplify relationships so as to make them more exploitable.

Here, I'll parse some of the ways in which this distance, as it manifests in the contemporary art world, is reified or dissolved by networks and modes of criticality. It seems to me that in both arenas it is imperative to constantly reassess the ways in which solidarity might be put to use.

If we take solidarity as an expression of morality, it is located not simply in the promotion of the idea of justice, but in acts. Avery Kolers has recently written of solidarity outside the terms of alliance, as deference to the judgment of those who suffer inequity. But it is important to properly account for the diverse and often-conflicting forms of inequity that complicate what that deference might look like. In the current climate, we might return to Émile Durkheim's theory of organic solidarity, which—in contrast to forms of cohesion based on labor, education, or kinship—refers to an interdependence based on specialization, or difference. It's a helpful model: solidarity as shared agency found not necessarily in shared intention, but in the production of a condition that assumes the necessity to constantly negotiate many different intentions. Chantal Mouffe's writing on agonism also comes to mind. She writes that true political thought is only made possible by accepting that complete inclusion and consensus are impossible. In an effort to establish modes of identification and representation that are in keeping with pluralism—the conditions in which we ostensibly want to find solidarity—we "must enable the expression of conflict."[4]

In a 2015 interview, Linda Nochlin admitted, "One of the things I did in the 70s was to study men ... they can take criticism. They do not burst into tears; they do not get all upset. Men say some really cutting, critical things about one another and that is acceptable. A level of confidence and an ability to take criticism is essential to success. Women all too often are not brought up to take intellectual and professional criticism, harsh criticism."[5] Here, we have a confounding object: A feminist art historian playing into a specious cliché about women's fragility—one that seems blithely impervious to the extremes of criticism constantly leveled at women, if only for their failures to meet impossible standards of femininity.

But nonetheless, I find myself wrestling with my own internalization of her remark. As a critic, I often try to check any impulse to be either too generous, gentle, and supportive, or too unsentimental and unsparing, when writing about the work of other women—specifically living women, and often emerging artists, who are the subject of 70 percent of my criticism over the past two years. And while I don't typically find that my writing veers in any of these directions to any unwarranted degree, the fact that I find myself looking for discrepancies gives those discrepancies some kind of shape, makes them real.

I suspect the problem isn't with women not being receptive to criticism; it's that critics may be hesitant to dole it out. The dominant approach to the practice of art criticism today, regardless of the gender of the artist—perhaps in response to the various encroachments on its charge by the curatorial text, the artist statement, the Facebook review, and Contemporary Art Daily—is to eschew the binaries of good and bad, or successful and unsuccessful. Instead, critics seek to offer something that augments the work being discussed, fleshing out a context that will position the work for a potential viewer and for posterity.

The idea is that the work has already been deemed worthy of attention by dint of it appearing in the limited real estate of a publication. In keeping with this ethos, a prevalent feminist methodology among women critics is quantitative, rather than qualitative. That is, the tactic plays out in terms of a percentage of coverage—or the number of women covered in relation to men—rather than on the level of language.

Johanna Fateman told me her fundamental critical strategy regarding women is to try to review perhaps more than 80 percent, and then in the writing to reflect her own intersectional feminist viewpoint and ideals. Prudence Peiffer echoed the sentiment. By covering many more female than male artists, she feels as though she is "working against certain blanket assumptions about art coverage." Kaelen Wilson-Goldie's approach shifts the focus from women to feminist artists: "I would like to think that I don't use different language or gender-specific language; I'm definitely not easier on women because they are women. As a critic I'm looking at what a feminist practice looks like and it's important to look for it in women and men's practices ... artists who deal with gender and power."

There are issues with both tactics. The Fateman/Peiffer approach recalls the problems inherent to any such affirmative action: To focus squarely on the work of women is, in some ways, to replicate the patriarchal gender binary that contributes to inequity. Wilson-Goldie's strategy, to prioritize feminist work without privileging the work of women, productively nuances the quantitative method. To do so takes the concept of organic solidarity at face value, leveraging collective agency through difference. But this treatment does not necessarily have the same blunt impact of contributing visibility, context, and capital to those who have been neglected by art's institutions and markets. A cynic might point to the fact that such treatment could normalize the appropriation and aestheticization of feminist discourse by those who might not ultimately have as much at stake.

Criticism, at its root, is an art of wielding power. We might look to Baudelaire, who claimed the practice "must be partial, passionate, and political, that is to say, written from an exclusive point of view, but a point of view that opens up the widest horizons." To open the widest horizons to a work, of course, is also to define the reach, the limit, of those horizons. Wilson-Goldie, discussing criticism in the context of both gender and region, said it directly: "It's not worth going off on something hard unless there is the power to sustain it." And therein lies the catch: If something can withstand the exertion of rigorous criticism that in many ways bestows power, it is often because the power was already there. A rigorous critique signals that the subject—the work, but ultimately the artist—is not only worthy enough of the attention to deserve a negative review, but powerful enough to survive it.

Take an obvious example regarding the apex of cynical extravagance—the recent *Art News* headline "A Disastrous Damien Hirst Show in Venice." The first lines of the article deem the show of 189 works, which cost upwards of 65 million dollars to produce, at the Palazzo Grassi and Punta della Dogana "one of the worst exhibitions of contemporary art staged in the past decade ... devoid of ideas, aesthetically bland, and ultimately snooze-inducing."[6] But this pan (and the myriad others like it) didn't halt sales or the spate of articles published on the work; articles which not only contributed to Hirst's already inflated cultural capital but also robbed artists with less exposure of the space on the page.

I don't mean to suggest that women critics have a responsibility to write unnecessarily harshly about the work of women artists. What I hope to convey is that the current trends in criticism, while evenhanded and generative, might unwittingly handicap artists who are already marginalized. Critique should, in the interest of promoting pluralism, be considered an act of solidarity. Too often in the context of women's efforts it is equated with bitchiness, cattiness, hostility. I think of Renata Adler, whose career became defined to some degree by her 8,000-word takedown, in 1980, of her *New Yorker* colleague Pauline Kael's collected writings, which she deemed to be "worthless" demagoguery. Rachel Cooke, writing in the *Guardian* in 2013, described the review as "journalistic sororicide." The issue isn't that there is a more entrenched divide between partiality and rivalry among women cultural producers. The issue is the *perception* that there is.

At the root of much of these conversations is the concession that empowerment is wrapped up in neoliberal capitalism and the pursuit of individual comfort and success, often at the expense of feminist pluralism. Because of that cultural emphasis, women in positions of power are not likely to try to dismantle the system that has benefited them, even as they acknowledge their positions as exceptions to the rule and their ascents as complicit in the patriarchy. "Individuals want the freedom to be a singularity and not have to represent an entire group or organization," Anicka Yi explained in a 2014 podcast titled "What Was Collaboration." "We want the freedom to fail, or be ourselves, to be post-identity politics .... A lot of females who are ambitious and intelligent have to be light on their feet and to cut themselves off from other people like them in order to succeed." Whereas Yi reckons with the complicated marriage of freedom and compromise that seems to attend this neoliberal success, in a separate conversation, Fateman articulated a similar discord in the ways in which successful women organize—it is often done with an aim of mobilizing an image of exceptionalism: "When you're dealing with people who do have a foothold in the art world, women organizing on the basis of being women is often kept secret—it's in a way uncool, an admission of a professional vulnerability. There is a reason that these things are separate and exclusive .... Obviously there's cachet to being the anomaly." It's a difficult charge, to be self-reflective about being the rewarded object of moral licensing—the psychological bargaining where one good deed excuses bad behavior. Anomalies don't alleviate discrimination, but they can justify the perpetuation of a discriminatory system. It's a fair question: Should those who come out on top have to risk hard-won privileges? Should they also be burdened with overturning the status quo?

If identity politics of the 80s and 90s was in part about facilitating alliances and communities, identity politics of today has illuminated, as Hannah Black has described, "the problem of establishing meaningful collectivity—without elision, domination, or uninflected hierarchy—against a capitalist class capable of extreme acts of violence and mass control. Collectivity might be the necessary first step toward making life bearable, but the production of that collectivity may be less cozy than strategies of inclusion, diversity, and universality suggest."[7] As we reimagine the ways in which forms of criticism and mentorship might better serve pathways to the kinds of success we privilege and collectivities that promote shared interests and standards, we must enable the expression of conflict. We cannot fear that it will result in rivalries or biases that will define us, limit us, make us exploitable. It is one thing to deny the existence of the art world's inequities, and it is another to write, to gather, and to produce as if they did not exist. There is a difference between not responding and stating a refusal to respond.

This article first appeared as Annie Godfrey Larmon, "Dirt Is Clean When There Is a Volume," *Apricota*, 2018.

1 Hannah Black, "The Identity Artist and the Identity Critic," *Artforum*, June 2016.

2 Maura Reilly, "Taking the Measure of Sexism: Facts, Figures, and Fixes," *Art News*, May 2015.

3 Suhail Malik, "Survey on Gender Ratios in Curating Programs," *Red Hook Journal*, October 23, 2012.

4 Chantal Mouffe, "Agonistic Democracy and Radical Politics," *Pavilion*, https://www.pavilionmagazine.org/chantal-mouffe-agonistic-democracy-and-radical-politics/.

5 Linda Nochlin, "Linda Nochlin on Feminism Then and Now," *Art News*, June 2015.

6 Andrew Russeth, "A Disastrous Damien Hirst Show in Venice," *Art News*, May 8, 2017.

7 Black, ibid.

SOFT TALK: THOUGHTS ON CRITIQUE

LESLIE DICK

One Tuesday evening in the Yale painting critique, where I was moonlighting as a visiting critic, I described a student's paintings as "truly weird." A moment later, another teacher said, "To tell you the truth, this soft talk drives me crazy." Leaving aside for a moment the ideology buried in the implied conflict between hard (good) and soft (crazy making), I want here to discuss critique as a theory and a practice, and to suggest that this thing dismissed so flippantly as *soft talk* might be a precious and productive resource.

One of the key elements of critique is the structural opposition between *interpretation* and *judgment*. What we do at art school is work towards becoming better artists, and making better art. Yet who defines what better art is? The authority figures—critics, curators, teachers, grant-giving bodies? The market? The dealers and the collectors? We can all think of examples where the art market seems to have been completely off in its assessments of value, where the authority figures seem out of touch and out of date. So what makes a better artwork?

The spectrum of success and failure does not hinge on the predilections of the critic or the pressures of the market; on the contrary, the success of a work is determined by the parameters set within the work itself. These parameters take form in specific elements, and we need to discuss and articulate how the artwork functions, what seems to be operative, what meanings emerge. Otherwise judgment (this worked, that didn't) seems to me like a power move, where I get to be the authority figure, and I get to say it's good, or better, or you've made progress, or you haven't.

We all unconsciously wish for authority figures; on some level, we want to believe that somewhere there is *one who knows*, one who can guarantee and validate our identities and our practices. But this is an illusion: the *one who knows* doesn't exist. Institutional structures tend to participate in this illusion, and to invite our participation. Within this framework, it is understood that there is something reassuring about hierarchies. Someone will judge your work, and it may be a harsh judgment this time around, but the basic structure (that there's an authority somewhere—in New York, perhaps—who knows what's good and what isn't) is sustained. The structure itself is a comforting illusion.

To work towards undoing this hierarchy is to create a situation that is much more unsettling—indeed, it can be a harsh awakening, opening up a radical space of uncertainty and vulnerability. At the same time, the artist may have deep respect for specific individuals, quite apart from their institutional authority, and that gives their words greater power. While it's a struggle for all of us to maintain a discourse constructed around uncertainty and vulnerability, ultimately I think it's more generative and more sustainable.

There are times in the critique when we want to make specific suggestions to the artist, or to make an evaluation. In this context, however, we are invested in the critical conversation, allowing complexity and contradiction through multiple voices, and so we put aside this advice for another time. Because otherwise it's cluttering up the task we are doing together there, which is to encounter and engage the work as it stands.

We engage the work on its terms by figuring out what those terms might be, and the work has to give us cues and clues, the instruments through which we engage it. It provides us with built-in *affordances*, handles to grasp, sequences to follow. Sometimes we find ourselves thinking about what the intentions of the artist might have been, as evidenced in the form and content of the work in front of us. I believe we engage in a creative hypothesis when we do this, imagining a hypothetical artist with hypothetical intentions. I don't believe it's particularly interesting or productive simply to ask the actual artists what they were thinking about, for a number of reasons, including the fact that they are not the best authority on their own work.

In my view, one of the points of this conversation is for the artist to find out how the work is operating: what meanings does it manifest? Are people moved by it? Does the artwork present its built-in affordances in a way that allows the curious and engaged viewer to interact with the work on its own terms? Asking the artist to tell us what she was thinking about may merely short-circuit both our process of discovery (which takes time and thought and rigor) and the possibility for the artist to find out what her artwork is doing.

Another reason not to treat artists, or anyone, as authorities on their own work is the existence of the unconscious, as well as the existence of social forces (ideology) in the form of discourses that flow through all of us, all the time. In other words, we're not in complete control of the meanings our works produce. Whatever we intended to put out there is exceeded by our unconscious thoughts and wishes, as well as by our social construction as subjects within discourse. Our autonomy as meaning-producers is informed by systems of representation and power that we did not invent and we do not control, and these systems are at work within us.

As artists, we may try as hard as we possibly can to control the meanings our artworks produce. At the same time, we acknowledge that we may have unwittingly materialized some other things that we did not consciously intend. We might inadvertently manifest class privilege, for example, or a wish to intimidate or impress; our work might display unconscious bias, or it might reiterate and repeat the racism of our world. The work may disclose our unconscious desires about our mother, which we thought we'd resolved some time ago. Or the work may address questions we weren't aware were in the mix, but in a positive way: it may expose relations of power in ways that propel viewers to question preconceived ideas, or produce a new awareness. In other words, the artwork always manifests *unconscious intentions*. The critical conversation allows for these unintended meanings to be discovered, as together we explore the ways the artwork is operating, the multiple meanings it generates, and the effects it produces.

In this process of interpretation and discovery, we must presume that every artistic decision that the artwork presents was (so to speak) intended. If we imagine that some things about the work are merely a mistake, then we protect ourselves from the obligation of actually engaging the artwork as it exists. Our task isn't to wonder about what could have been done differently, but rather to interact and engage with the work in front of us, and therefore to assume that the work is the most compelling work it can be. Assuming that some of the elements in the work are simply a technical error (or an error of judgment on the part of the artist) allows us to sidestep the task of describing and understanding how those elements operate.

It is much more challenging to assume the best of the artwork. It is harder to begin by defending the work. In my view, anything that seems like a technical failure is better approached as a formal element in the artwork. I try to look at the work as if it's already valid, or already accepted as a successful artwork. That helps me get past my preconceived ideas of what a successful artwork looks like.

Sometimes when I'm grappling with understanding how an artwork is operating, I think about how the artwork proposes a viewing subject (a position from which the artwork may be viewed and, so to speak, understood) that may not coincide with my actual subjectivity. In viewing, I temporarily occupy the subject position of the ideal viewer of this artwork, in order to engage it. Then I step outside that perspective, to bring those perceptions into my own subjective field.

When I engage the artwork in this way, inevitably I find myself wondering about the artist's intentions. In doing so, I am constructing a presumed artist, imagining a maker who had intentions, who may in turn be a fiction, an inauthentic persona constructed by the actual artist, whose subjectivity exceeds this position. In other words, just as I temporarily occupy the subject position of the *viewer*, and then regain my own complex and contradictory subjectivity, so too does the hypothetical artist, who makes a work that implies the subject position of the *maker*, and then moves on to make another work, which may imply a radically different position and point of articulation.

We are aware that we are not dealing with actual people here: we are dealing with implied, temporary positions, projected by the artwork, in order to discuss the work in a zone of hypothesis. We ask: what if the artist intended us to think or feel this? We don't check with the actual artists here, even if they're in the room. We check with the artwork, to see if it holds the formal and material elements that would produce that thought and feeling. The question becomes, what does the artwork intend us to think or feel, or maybe, what is the artwork asking of us, what is it inviting us to do?

I am describing a critical practice, of hypothetical thinking and presumed temporary relations, which is infused with doubt and uncertainty. It is also a space of vulnerability, as we all feel vulnerable when we enter into such a precarious discourse. Authoritarian critical discourse shuts down the possibilities that this space might open up, by reestablishing an implied figure, the *one who knows*, and guaranteeing that our uncertainty has a limit. In my view, the limit to uncertainty is the work itself—its material form—and we engage it through discourse.

Part of what makes *soft talk* possible is time. If there's plenty of time, there's an openness that allows for uncertainty—a kind of suspension of certainty, and certainly a suspension of judgment. At CalArts, Michael Asher's critique classes continued until there was nothing more to say. If someone wanted to revisit a thought that had come up hours before, the group continued the conversation. Through circling back, taking time, through repetition and working through, a form in language was built up, not equivalent to the artwork, but coextensive with it.

I believe that what we are committed to doing together is making an exciting, generative, productive conversation around what may be not very good artwork. This isn't primarily driven by a wish to help the artist make better artwork, although that could be a by-product of the conversation. We do it to make us better at looking and interpreting and responding to new ideas and new forms that may unsettle and disturb us. We do it to bring words to these forms. And it can make us better artists and viewers, because through this process we can begin to have a better understanding of how artworks operate.

As for *soft talk*, I like it. I like the implication that we're maybe doing something gooey and awkward and generous, and that our discourse gives, like a pillow, rather than cuts, like a knife. And part of what I want to suggest is that there are ways to think about rigor in the *soft talk* that we are doing. I believe that being able to point to the precise material elements in the artwork that produce the sensation of "weirdness" (or any other response) is how we focus the conversation on the specifics of the work. I believe that our conversation has to be anchored in the materiality of the work in front of us; otherwise it can indeed veer off into unstructured reminiscences of banal feelings. But as someone deeply invested in psychoanalytic theory, I do not use the term "free association" pejoratively. Freud's practice of "free association" is far from free, because following the chain of associations brings us to deeper meanings that we cannot access otherwise. It's unrelenting, the way free association takes us there. So following our thoughts (while staying located in the formal and material qualities of the specific artwork) takes us places we might otherwise never go, and allows for something to be revealed.

It's paradoxical. As artists we may work towards controlling the meanings produced by the artwork with great intensity and intention; we tighten the screws on structures of representation and materiality, trying to limit and direct the possible readings of the work. Yet it is precisely in this tightly controlled work that inadvertent affects and effects squeeze out the edges. What we didn't intend is often a crucial part of the final work, and the more intentional we are in our practice, the more these by-products ooze out and come into being. That seems to me like a good thing.

For me, what's exciting about artworks is the way that meanings proliferate: that unintended leakage and ooze at the level of meaning is generative and alive. New contexts make new meanings happen: a performance in a prison, or a factory, or an airport, or in a different decade literally operates differently. I see artworks as mechanisms for generating meaning. I'm thrilled by the process of following up on those meanings and pointing to the precise formal and material and contextual elements that produced them.

I am personally less interested in locating the artwork within the history of contemporary art (although that may be an important dimension of the work) than I am in understanding how the work engages the specific context of our historical moment. I am intrigued by the presumption that all worthwhile artworks are somehow engaged in a process of critiquing the dominant ideological and political formations of our time. At CalArts, that's called "criticality," and the cry goes up, "Where's the criticality?" Some people believe that's what validates an artwork, or invalidates it. I think there are many ways to challenge received ideas and power structures, and sometimes refusing to engage dominant ideology directly can be a way of carving out another space for discourse and experience. Sometimes the artwork steps aside from explicit "criticality," in order to do something else, something other. But I am also convinced that there's no space outside the power structures of our world, so inevitably we speak a language that participates in the oppressive ideologies of racism, capitalism, the patriarchy, even when our work proposes an elsewhere. In this context, the *other thing* the artwork may be doing will be temporary and precarious, and those qualities are precious and worth articulating.

There are, needless to say, multiple strategies to make the critical conversation productive and exciting. Bringing in literary and pop culture references, making connections to other artists of the past or the present, finding the underlying discursive interconnections within the work are all approaches we value and pursue. At CalArts, when I started teaching there in the early 1990s, the dominant mode of critique was to ask the artists to explain their intentions in as much detail as possible, and then to use that verbal explanation almost like evidence in a courtroom, measuring those stated intentions against the artwork itself. It was productive in that it helped the artists see how far their artworks had drifted from their conscious stated intentions. Yet that drift was seen as a problem, and artists were slammed for producing work that didn't line up with their words. Bringing language to bear on the artwork was a way to build a case, using the artists' own words against them. It was brutal. It also avoided the risk of hypothetical thinking, that is, the risk of entering a zone where the artist's stated intentions are temporarily set aside.

Without the artist's instruction or direction, we can venture into a space of uncertainty, where viewers wonder what is going on with this particular artwork and together find words to make an account of the work, slowly building a discursive form that can hold the multiple meanings the work generates. I believe that drift and divergence are not only inevitable, but also of great value, as they open up a possibility for the artist, and viewer, to find out something that's true, that we didn't already know. When I do a studio visit with an artist, this is my wish: to uncover, in the conversation together, something that's true about the work, that hasn't yet been recognized. It's a very uncertain process, but sometimes I know when we've got there: a silence falls, a moment of reflection. This possibility of discovery (through the making and the discussion of the work) keeps me coming back to the critique, to this endless exchange, where we try to articulate the ways that artworks operate and generate meaning and, in weaving together these different conversations, to sustain a precarious and ever-changing community.

This essay first appeared as Leslie Dick, "Soft Talk: Thoughts on Critique," *X-TRA* 21, no. 1 (Fall 2018), https://www.x-traonline.org/article/soft-talk-thoughts-on-critique.

MIRA DAYAL: Leslie, your essay "Soft Talk" was prompted by a studio critique. You begin by reclaiming this phrase that another professor used—lamenting "soft talk" in your critique—as a framework for thinking about a model for criticism, something generous, progressive, and supportive. Annie, in your essay, "Dirt Is Clean When There Is a Volume," you set up a relationship between the ideas of celebration and solidarity. Because those terms carry preexisting associations, could you elaborate on how you came to position those two terms in relationship to each other in your essay?

ANNIE GODFREY LARMON: The essay opens with an anecdote about having commissioned a short text by Jo Baer for an issue of *Artforum* for a section dedicated to Agnes Martin. When Jo responded to my email, in short, she refused to respond—she called Martin out as bitchy and said, "I know women artists are supposed to be in solidarity, but even in death?" We decided to run her reply because it in fact was a very strong statement about the ways in which those two artists have been historicized together by certain circumstances outside of their own interests. I wrote the piece for *Apricota* after a prompt from Andrianna Campbell and Joanna Fiduccia to write about fights. This was coming at a moment after the *Artforum* issue on identity politics was published and we were thinking about such themes as they've been updated from conversations in the late 80s and early 90s. I developed my ideas for this essay in the period leading up to the Women's March. Around the same time, Anicka Yi's *Lonely Samurai* podcast came out; with Amy Sillman, Ruba Katrib, Stefania Bortolami, and Andrew Russeth, she spoke about the viability of female networks in the art world, cronyism, what a female-oriented cronyism might look like, and how mentorships play out among women in the art world. I was also speaking with a number of my women colleagues about women artists and how to show solidarity, to support young or historically under-recognized artists' work. Is there any difference in the way that we see the critical framework when the agenda is presumably to help bring attention or resources to an artist?

All of these things were in the background when I was conceiving this piece, and I kept coming back to this term, *solidarity*, and thinking about how Jo was saying, "Do I need to celebrate Agnes Martin's work?" I wanted to hash out some of those issues and also think about this "ick" factor that comes up when you talk about being a "woman artist" or "woman curator"—people often don't want to participate in that strict category, and

I wanted to unpack why. Is it because of conversations about intersectional feminism, where we understand that these things are much more nuanced? Is it about not wanting to play into essentializing stereotypes? Not wanting to marginalize oneself?

I thought about solidarity through Émile Durkheim's notion of organic solidarity. He writes about a model of mechanical solidarity that is based on homogeneous interests—union over shared work, shared education, shared gender—whereas organic solidarity involves coming together for heterogeneous reasons, because of difference. The latter is used to describe industrial modern societies wherein work is specialized; we're interdependent because we rely on each other to make the bigger picture. So, thinking of Durkheim, and Chantal Mouffe and Ernesto Laclau's concept of agonism—the idea that democracy cannot exist without conflict, and that we need to make space for conflict—I decided to think about solidarity and criticism coming together as a union over the production of the space in which conflict is assumed. I wrote about what I see as trends in criticism right now, where, for example, the text is focused on augmenting the context of an artist's work or providing very generous readings, which I myself fall into. These are examples of writing alongside an artist as opposed to relying on the very banal binary of good and bad.

LESLIE DICK: The essay is really interesting because, for me, there is absolutely no question that feminism is a space of conflict, debate, contradiction, and complexity, and that there is no single definition of what solidarity would look like. The fact that women artists don't make as much money as men artists do, or that women artists don't show in the same galleries, or get the same number of museum shows—these are all parameters that we are all very, very familiar with, but in a sense, my essay is not about that at all. It's not about power in the art world, or compensation in the art world, or even recognition in the art world. My essay comes not out of a practice of art criticism but a practice of teaching. So my essay is about what we call crits, which is when a bunch of people sit down and try to talk about an artwork together. I wrote it because I had this fascinating moment where I was invited to participate in a painting crit at Yale School of Art a few years ago, and I tried to talk about the content of the work rather than the form. I said something slightly idiotic: "This painting seems really weird to me." I had that teacherly hope that if I said something slightly idiotic, the students might say something, they might speak up, hesitantly, provisionally, instead of these teachers who lay down the law so emphatically. And one of those teachers responded, "To tell you the truth, this soft talk is driving me crazy."

I was so insulted that I took the phrase soft talk and decided to write about what I think a crit is for, to break it down. I've taught at CalArts since 1992, and a huge proportion of what we do is either alone in the studio with the artist or in a group conversation. I tried to describe what the conversation is for, what strategies we bring to it, and how to make it work. For me, one of the most fundamental things I was trying to say was that we all want there to be an authority figure somewhere, "the one who knows." If you're a painter, and you make a painting, and the teacher walks in and says it's not good for this reason, and this reason, and this reason, that may be harsh. But next time, that authority figure might give you the validation that you're looking for.

So the idea that a singular authority figure might exist—the dad, the judge, the law, the thing beyond us—can be reassuring. But I don't believe in the "one who knows" because I don't believe in the market and I don't believe in reputation. I think that there are many, many artists who are making incredible work outside that frame. For me, the question is not whether the work is good or bad, because I am committed to questioning whatever value systems prop up those judgments.

My question is, how is the sculpture operating? What is it asking me to do? How do I have to bend and dance with it to understand how it is generating meaning? I'm not interested in the artist telling me that. I'm not interested in the authority figure telling me that. I'm interested in the group conversation where we all look very carefully and do close readings, where we're responding and reacting and putting into language a relationship to an artwork. I don't think it's easy, but it tips the balance away from judgment (and a commercial art world market value of what constitutes success) toward interpretation.

"Soft talk" is a precious resource. I almost felt like I could stop teaching after I wrote the essay because I hoped people would be able to use it and also react to it, respond to it, and maybe say, "That's not what I do, no, no, no, you're wrong." And in fact, some of the students told me, "We want judgment, we want someone to tell us that painting's good, and that one isn't. We're desperate for it. We need it." Judgment is inevitable. It's all part of the process, but it's good to lean away from the notion that I, as the teacher who's been teaching for many years, know what a better artwork would be. I'm always joking with the students: I say, you know, you've bothered to spend all this money to come to school to become better artists, so who knows what a better artist is? And of course it comes down to, "Well, that teacher is my hero, and he must know, or she must know"—or, "This gallerist must know." In my view, the only person who knows is the artist. The artist is the only person who can say, "I made these paintings last October, and now it's April, and I think these paintings are better than those paintings."

AUDIENCE: But why?

LD: Exactly. Precisely why, and why is more interesting to me. I'm always arguing that the crit conversation is not for the artist. It's not a message to the artist saying, "You could have done it, you know, if you turned it upside down, maybe—I mean, what about green underneath? Maybe it should be blue ... " You know, providing suggestions, alternatives, prompts to adjust this thing so that it becomes more what I think it should be, and the artist is maybe taking notes. To me, the value is in the conversation itself. If the artist hears something that helps them, great. But let's talk about it as if the artist weren't in the room. Let's talk about it as if our task is to have a really good conversation. And what's weird about the art critic is that, in a sense, they're having that conversation with an imaginary group, people who read the text.

ON QUEER FEMINIST CRITIQUE

TAUSIF NOOR

I don't think I knew what art criticism was until I started writing it; certainly, I didn't know any art critics, nor what the job entailed. I studied art history in college and learned over time how to look closely at objects—to not only describe but analyze, assess and ascertain meanings, values, virtues, and so on. I can't say that this naiveté was particularly beneficial, but I have been tremendously lucky in that my very first editors and readers, all artists, friends, and mentors, were all unfailingly kind.

Each of those people has also contributed in some way to the expansive and illuminating ethos of what I see as queer feminist criticism, the framework that has facilitated so much of my thinking. I'll stress here that while not all these people would identify as queer or as queer feminists, they have all imparted its central lesson: that the problem of *not knowing* is instead a problem of what it means to know at all. For a while, what *not knowing* meant for me was not knowing *how* to translate what I felt or saw or understood about art into text that felt engaging; as I write more, it has become a matter of learning how to trust my own judgments, how to be honest. These days, I find myself trying to take what I have learned from queer feminists to try to write with the kind of urgency and empathy that drew me to this field in the first place.

What a queer feminist mode of critique has entailed for me as a writer is working through all the incidents when what I ostensibly hope to *assess* or *analyze* squirms away, fleeing my attempts to pin it down, to say the *right* thing. While writing about performances where the bodies of the performers are put at risk of real, physical injury, or about paintings that redefine kitsch and bad taste, or on films that suture the sublime and the grotesque, I am placed in a position wherein I confront my prejudices, the limits of my understanding, and the bounds of my knowledge. I think it's important to do your research as a critic, to understand the terrain of what you wish you comment on, but practically speaking, I know that research is my main form of procrastination, an exercise in avoidance disguised as productivity. It's natural to want to know everything before you form your own opinions, and an informed opinion is better than its counterpart, but research can also instill paranoia. It's far better, and easier, to approach writing criticism with the conviction that every assignment, every essay, no matter the subject, will teach you something you didn't plan to learn.

By queer feminist criticism, then, I mean criticism that renounces any separation of the affective from the political, that is less interested in *excavating*, *uncovering*, or *denuding* its object from the mysteries shrouding it than in posing questions about the value, labor, and circulation of art right alongside questions of sensation, solidarity, and attachment. When confronted with art—whether objects, experiences, or the loose ends of sensations instantiated by people who seek to shift the registers of our perception in some way, however small—the critic who takes seriously the project of queer feminism is obligated to allow for the possibility that the very frameworks with which they are armed to *assess* and *analyze* may in fact be completely futile.

I don't mean to advocate for an unfettered surrender to the mysticism of art, nor do I think that queer feminism is all about epistemic humility. Much of what drives me to continue reading and writing criticism is the understanding that criticism doesn't serve to affirm what I already know or believe to be true. I find such a mode of criticism both desultory and stultifying in its smug refusal to admit that what art does best is to take us in directions previously unplanned and leave us with questions rather than answers.

For so long, my aesthetic judgments—my purported "taste"—defined a key part of my character, but when I found myself weeping at the end of a tour of a lesbian feminist haunted house, or talking to a group of artists who recounted their time marching through the streets with video cameras to force the government to acknowledge the AIDS crisis, and then trying to find the words to capture those experiences, I recognized that there was so much I had yet to learn about art, about criticism, about myself. These were people who encouraged me to continue asking the questions that guide me today. I'm still trying to get it right.

LINDSAY PRESTON ZAPPAS: MOCA advertises every issue on *Carla*'s back cover, and once I wrote a very critical review of an Adrian Villar Rojas show there. The curator actually emailed me to say that it was the best review he had read. On that scale, they can take it. It's the smaller galleries that will email with feedback. But in general, the community in LA is pretty responsive.

AMY FUNG: And you can tell that person cared…

LPZ: Right. I love what you said about criticism being a generous act. My "harshest" reviews are often of shows that I really liked. In the process of thinking and writing, you produce some critical resistance.

MIRA DAYAL: In order to write a relatively successful negative review, you have to lay out the terms and engage with the work to defend your critique, because a negative review often has to position itself in a defensive way, to show it is merited. Those negative reviews can be the most successful or thorough.

LPZ: We've gotten into some hot water when writers don't do the work you're talking about, when they don't build up the argument enough to be critical. I think it's dangerous and irresponsible to publish something where the writer didn't do the work to bolster the critique enough, because that encourages a type of top-down criticism, and I don't believe in that kind of authority. Criticality needs to be supported and fleshed out.

NEUTRALITY AND FEMINISM
WENDY VOGEL

As a critic who regularly writes exhibition reviews, I have a strict rule against covering artist friends in this format. Many art world colleagues are surprised that I stick to this mandate. Some have argued that critical objectivity died long ago. Others wonder why I, as a critic committed to feminist practice, don't want to review artists in my social circle. Rather than a limitation, I see this stance of critical neutrality *as* a feminist act.

I define neutrality not as the opposite of a politicized orientation, but rather as a lack of personal entanglement with an artist. Remaining neutral does not, however, equate to making a definitive evaluation based on formal criteria alone. By approaching an artist's practice from a neutral perspective, I aim to bring a new outlook or set of references to the work beyond the artist's intentions. In some instances, that might involve antagonism or a direct challenge; at other times, that might mean expanding the historical context around the work. In both cases, distance (a degree of unfamiliarity with the work, a need to figure out how the practice could be positioned, a lack of anticipated interpersonal repercussions) is helpful. I think of criticism as plurality, as abundance—an action in line with lived feminism, which ultimately champions expansiveness.

As with most of my feminist principles, I came to this conclusion through personal experience. I began writing criticism in the years immediately following the Great Recession. In the fall of 2009, I moved to Houston to participate in a two-year residency program for artists and critics. The art market at the time, especially in Texas, favored traditionally sellable objects as the economy recovered. Despite revived interest in Conceptual and performance art, work that addressed racial, gender, and sexual oppression could still be dismissed by the phrase "identity politics." The term, weaponized since the 1990s, suggested a topical stridency that would not stand the test of time.

"Identity politics" also connoted an emotional pull or one-note moralism at odds with the supposed toughness of radical art. The *Los Angeles Times* critic Christopher Knight's infamous review of the 1993 Whitney Biennial put it bluntly: "Forget 'multicultural' or 'politically correct.' This is the Patronizing Biennial, brought to you by the Therapeutic Museum." Knight argued that "in the United States, the single most conventional idea about art is that it ought to be good for you." He snubbed art that openly critiqued racism and sexism as pedantic "Vitamin C for the soul."

I have always vehemently disagreed with Knight: I see institutional and political critique as the opposite of "conventional." But as a young critic and editor, I internalized all the ways in which I—and the identity-focused work I wished to champion—might be perceived as soft, emotional, and therefore dismissible. Striking an authoritative yet politicized tone can still be challenging for those who identify as other than cis male: too tough and you're disgruntled, too encouraging, a cheerleader. In my early days, I wrote plenty of positive reviews, unsullied by social ties. I also honed my negative reviewing chops, hacking out my feminist stance in the process. In 2011, I delivered a damning opinion of Laurel Nakadate's MOMA PS1 retrospective for the journal *Pastelegram*, writing that the artist "[skims] the surface of bad-girl feminism with a heavy dose of exploitation." I claimed that her work fell too easily into the category of commodifiable "self-objectification." All the while, I worried about being perceived as a sanctimonious scold.

While I grappled with how to practice feminism in my critical writing, I noticed an irritating Texas trend of promoting male-dominated artist collectives. My frustration boiled over in a 2011 article published in *Temporary Art Review*. Fresh off a breakup with a male artist, I spun a review of the performance duo Harrison & Wood into a meta-meditation on boys' club art (all while nursing a delusional hope for reconciliation—my lede mentions "my artist boyfriend" charitably, in present tense). To date, this is one of the only pieces where I twisted unrequited libidinal investment into rage. My essay targets, among other groups, a local dicks-and-tits zine drawing collective. They "blithely re-appropriate feminist language in calling their group a 'quilting club for men,'" I wrote. While I stand by that statement, I may have gone a bit far in calling out a museum curator for endorsing "bro-ish pranksterism under the guise of mass appeal." In this instance, my personal investment in the subject skewed my political orientation toward vendetta.

Before this commission, I hadn't revisited either piece in nearly a decade. Despite the cringey moments of posturing, I am proud of the clarity and risk-taking in these articles. It is often more difficult to convey such directness while reviewing from a position of feminist neutrality—to tease out one's own argument about the work without starting from an outsize emotional reaction. It is ultimately rewarding for both the writer and the artist, however. I have challenged myself to search for unfamiliar work and artists, bonded in person with former review subjects, and sought out opportunities to write in longer formats or in less conventional ways about the artists who are also friends. In this last case, where critical distance is not possible, I follow and expand on the artist's intentions—in the best circumstances approaching a kind of intellectual collaboration.

WRITING

FORM, STYLE, AND VOICE

How do writers decide what form to use to address a particular artwork?

Where does the "I" come into art criticism?

How can conversational forms push against hierarchical structures within art criticism?

How do writers determine who their audience is and how to communicate with them?

WRITING IN RELATION
RE'AL CHRISTIAN

I do not often refer to myself as a critic. The word *critic* stems from the Latin *criticus*, meaning "judge," which might imply a certain level of condemnation or hierarchy. As a writer, I have never felt it was my position to judge an artist's work; I find camaraderie between myself and the artist. People often think in terms of "I," and therefore find it difficult to understand how others think, or to imagine how another individual processes the world, especially when their process does not immediately align with one's own. When I write, I don't presume to be an authority on an artist's work, or to establish a dominating opinion, an overwhelming "I." Instead, I write to create a dialogue between myself (and by extension the reader) and the artist. I also write to understand a particular way of moving about the world, of navigating social realities through an artistic lens.

There are many ways to relate to an artist's work—through a shared identity, through a relationship to space and place. As a writer of color, I am often drawn to artists who have experienced diaspora in one way or another; I aim to find connections. In this way, I find criticism to be a form of empathy, and this empathy to be a powerful antidote, or a means of pushing against, a form of writing that prioritizes a supposedly "objective" opinion. I can't imagine that a critic would ever claim to be entirely objective, yet neutrality is often perceived as a virtue. But for a critic to claim neutrality is itself a political move that positions the writer as the majority, a voice that embodies the hegemonic gaze. Their personal opinions become elusive and slippery as they widen the distance between themselves, the artist, and of course the reader.

In my own process, I consider how intimacy within writing might make room for more voices, creating a space for others to enter, not by asserting an argument, but by approaching the act of writing as a process of looking, understanding difference, and putting oneself in relation with another. I'm drawn to the world-building potential of empathetic writing, which I find in the work of writers like James Baldwin, Joan Didion, bell hooks, and Barbara Christian. This excerpt from Baldwin's "Autobiographical Notes" (1955) for example, epitomizes the writer's style in a few simple lines:

> One writes out of one thing only—one's own experience. Everything depends on how relentlessly one forces from this experience the last drop, sweet or bitter, it can possibly give. This is the only real concern of the artist, to recreate out of the disorder of life that order which is art. The difficulty then, for me, of being a Negro writer was the fact that I was, in effect, prohibited from examining my own experience too closely by the tremendous demands and the very real dangers of my social situation.

The text is clean, rhythmic, written as though it were being spoken, the punctuation holding space for gaps and pauses in his dialogue with the reader. The cool, critical distance of the third-person pronoun, "one," is quickly followed by the intimacy of the first-person "me"; Baldwin intentionally undercuts his own objectivity to reveal a brutally honest truth. This passage, like much of his other writing, leads me to wonder what has been left out—how the gaps, pauses, and punctuation aid his lyrical rhythm, but also hold space for poetic omissions. There is more to be said, but he holds back. His meaning is clear, but in those pauses he leaves us to wonder, inviting us into the world of the text to better understand his perspective.

Through empathetic writing, we can better understand and immerse ourselves in the new worlds that artists create to confront the many disorders in our world. Artists may offer spacious invitations to the viewer, just as Baldwin does to the reader, but similarly the questions they ask of us may not have easy answers. My responsibility as a writer is not necessarily to answer their questions, but to create spaces in which we can grapple with them, knowing, as a Black woman writer, the potential of my empathy being the lens through which we see the world.

MIRA DAYAL: Something I've been thinking about in this conversation series as a whole is reframing these concerns to think about who this writing is *for*—who are you writing *to* when you are writing? That small shift in phrasing enables me to think about writing not just for this void, this editor, this publication, but for this artist. What do I want to tell this artist about their work that excites me and hasn't been talked about already? How can this piece of writing help the artist, even if it isn't critical? Of course, sometimes, being critical is the most helpful thing I can do for an artist. Jess, you've brought up intimacy as it relates to criticism and intellectual partnerships with artists. I want to talk more about the formal aspect of your writing—it has often taken an epistolary form. This can be a way of talking *around* art, as Merray has put it, but it is also an intimate form, and a way of pointing to a specific audience or addressee.

JESSICA LYNNE: The letter offers so much. I learned to appreciate the letter through the artists I consider myself in intellectual partnership with. [Names specifically Chloë Bass and Kameelah Janan Rasheed, who are in the audience.] This form tries to meet the form of the artist. I want to write in real time, for myself and for the artist, but also for posterity. I want to embed a sense of futurity in the work. The letter does a lot of those things. Beyond that, I'm generally bored with how criticism works. I'm bored by a lot of what I read. I want to read things that take chances. Poets teach us how to do that. Good essayists teach us how to do that. I try really hard as an editor at *ARTS.BLACK* to allow folks to take the space to do that. What will keep me excited about art criticism? I studied fiction in school and really loved some of those moments in a workshop where, even if a text wasn't working, someone was trying to think differently about the words on the page. Writing an approximation of a different thing makes me feel good. The artists I'm most inspired by and committed to are also thinking about form.

MD: Merray, would you like to talk about these concerns in your writing, which you describe as "writing around art"?

MERRAY GERGES: I didn't learn how to write when I studied art history. I learned how to write when I studied journalism, and I was studying art history at the same time. I was three years into the art history program and I didn't know how to write. From very early on, I felt that there was a tension between journalism and the art world. My practice is rooted in trying to find common ground between these two disciplines.

"Writing around" is a term I only began to use recently. While I was in J-school, I found myself losing interest in art. For my thesis project, I had found traces of this gallery in Halifax that was around in the late 90s, called the Multicultural Arts Resource Centre, which helped new immigrants find artistic resources and gave them space to show their work. I went on this treasure hunt trying to find out why I hadn't heard of this and who had been involved in it. I managed to find them, and they were both Black Nova Scotians who had been doing so much work for so long, but their work wasn't in the official records. When I started to publish my writing, I was more interested in looking at the systems within which art circulated, or did not, and within which it was discussed, or not, rather than the art itself. So much of that early writing came from how I moved through these systems. I am implicated in them too. And I felt that this writing wasn't taken seriously.

This goes back to what people expect you to write and how they expect you to write it. Last year, I wrote an essay about Kapwani Kiwanga, about a show that she had done in a small regional gallery in Quebec. She had extracted a strip of dirt from the front of the museum and put this pile of dirt in the middle of the space. Viewers were asked to use a clay scoop to return the dirt to where it was taken from. The work alludes to practices of repatriation and acknowledges the Indigenous land that the gallery is situated on. I happened to walk in on an elderly white Quebecois couple being led through the show by an elderly white Quebecois tour guide, and these people were engaging with the show as if it were a joke. I asked the tour guide if people actually did what they were asked to do with the work, and she said, "Yeah, children do, but adults don't." I asked her why she thought that was the case, and she said, "Because adults only do things that are useful."

The piece I wrote was only 1,000 words long, and it was basically a description of this scene. For me, it was really clear that I was giving an example of how the audience engaged with the work to say that the work didn't *work* in the context within which it was supposed to. I could have spelled it out, but I was using a very basic journalistic technique called show, don't tell. When the essay came out, people reacted like, "I read your piece—what were you trying to say? What did you think of the work?" Kiwanga's work is about exposing the insidious apparatuses of systems and how they regulate the bodies that move through them, and I felt that I was trying to do the same thing with my writing. I told Kiwanga, I'm doing what you're doing—I'm looking at the structure. She responded that I was talking "*around* the work." We don't talk enough about the way a show is written about or the way it's received and how that relates to the work itself.

ART CRITICISM AND THE ETHICS OF AESTHETICS: WRITING ON RICHARD MOSSE'S *THE ENCLAVE*

YANIYA LEE

My first attempts at writing about Richard Mosse's *The Enclave* (2012–13) were poor. I saw the video installation in the fall of 2014, at DHC/ART Foundation for Contemporary Art in Montreal. The Irish artist used expired infrared film, a military technology that turns greens into reds with striking effect, to capture the landscape and people of the Democratic Republic of Congo (DRC). The six-channel installation was projected onto free-floating double-sided screens and immersed in an amplified original score. It was impossible to see all the screens at once, which forced you to move throughout the forty-minute span of the videos, never sure what you had missed. Brief, pink-tinted slow pans and wide shots overlapped: a group of people move a house; a woman's stomach is sliced open to retrieve a baby; young men jump through hoops of fire; a man walks into a body of water and disappears. The maelstrom of fragments refused to coalesce into a cohesive narrative for the intended Western audiences. What we were offered was anxiety. Inside *The Enclave*, untethered to any contextual information, the Congolese people were presented as unintelligible. I am rarely moved by exhibitions, but as I experienced *The Enclave*, I became increasingly uncomfortable, angry, and physically sick.

Most reviews and writing about the work, which premiered at the Irish Pavilion at the 2013 Venice Biennale, were either positive or shallow, focused on the visual effects of the film and never delving into the disjuncture between the artist's intentions and the work's implications. To me, these stunning images were violent because Mosse infused his fungible African subjects with his own racial anxiety. What *The Enclave* re-created, and what the beauty of the work obfuscated, was the unease and confusion that Mosse and his crew experienced on their return visits to the DRC. Unfortunately, when I first saw the work, I didn't have the vocabulary to express what felt so wrong about the installation.

In a pitch I sent to the editor of an online publication, I wrote, "The forty-minute video installation is mesmerizing and devastating and ultimately very upsetting. What is the ethical responsibility of the privileged, white, male, European artist presenting documentary images of an abstracted civil war in the Congo to a predominantly Western audience, in an art context? *The Enclave*'s overwhelming beauty makes it hard to extricate and pin down exactly why it's problematic, and I'd like to take the time to figure out why." Looking back on the email thread, I see large gaps in our correspondence. I had struggled to find the right words to articulate my criticism. I submitted a final draft several months after my initial pitch, only to have it promptly rejected by the editor. "You've demonstrated great tenacity, confidence, ambition, and modesty in this process, and I'm impressed and grateful for your measure of composure and constancy during this exchange," she wrote. "However it isn't going to work, I'm sorry. This text would require too much editing, still."

Undaunted, I kept thinking about *The Enclave* and the physical reaction it had provoked in me, not because of how the installation looked but *how it had been made*. "I was trying to make visible this very overlooked conflict," Mosse said in several interviews. He claimed to have made this film to bring attention to the ongoing, unseen, "cancerous cycle of vicious little wars" in Congo.[1] The way Mosse uses surveillance technology makes race *invisible,* even while the Black experience is one of hypervisibility (and consequent vulnerability) due to racialization. This was an outrageous reversal, considering the experience represented in Mosse's artwork was actually his own and not that of his subjects.

That fall, I started graduate school, and there I attempted once again to write about the installation, this time within an academic context. I brought in theory and philosophy, cited Saidiya Hartman, Christina Sharpe, and Edward Said. The essay was more than 5,000 words long and overwrought with theory and analysis. It had an academic tone in place of an open, straightforward presentation of the problems in Mosse's work. I had not yet resolved what was disturbing about the installation. A few months later, I repositioned my critique through the lenses of colonialism and surveillance and shared it at a moving image research forum. The presentation went well, but my initial physical reaction was obscured by the interesting histories I had uncovered in my research.

A few years later, I was invited to be a writer-in-residence at a photography gallery. I finally wrote about Mosse's exhibition in a satisfying way. My mandate was clear during that residency: I set out to think about images ethically. *The Enclave* was a perfect subject. Part essay, part review, and told through a personal perspective, this final attempt succeeded because of its combination of approaches. It was authentic, clear, and simple. *The Enclave* was not a film about the DRC. I wrote about the "shadowy side of white imagination, where the cognitive dissonance that fostered a European sense of superiority endures," and how "the faces and movements of the people in the work, their bodies and rituals, were abstracted and presented to illustrate the artist's fearful sentiment." I wrote about deceitful images and the social hierarchies of a world shaped by empire. I discussed the materiality and methodology of photography and of my own critique of *The Enclave.* I asked, *Does this matter?* If so, *Why does it matter?* And, *To whom does it matter?* My language was personal, precise, descriptive, and analytic. In a way that none of my previous attempts had succeeded to do, this text brought together all the components I needed for a full discussion of the problematic work. In the end, this final iteration of writing, after a long struggle with words and vocabulary, was my triumphant response to the brutality of Mosse's unethical aesthetics.

I am grateful for this four-year encounter with *The Enclave*. The work presented a challenge that prompted me to grow as a writer until I was able to confront its complications. It propelled me to try articulating my critique in all sorts of venues/formats—an art criticism blog, an academic paper, a public lecture, and a personal essay. Each version brought out a new aspect of my criticism until the research and revision of my attention to *The Enclave* had pushed me to an expanded vocabulary, with which I could describe and analyze what I saw, as well as the effect the work had beyond the artist's intention. I discovered that materialist criticism requires rigor, and that ethical considerations must be discussed within the appropriate context and with the right vocabulary in order to justly point out representational violence or (hopefully more often) celebrate liberatory creative practices.

1 Richard Mosse and John Kelly, "Richard Mosse | Extended Interview | The Works | RTÉ ONE," February 14, 2014, in *The Works*, RTÉ ONE, 11:56, https://www.youtube.com/watch?v=QbSDv-5v_x4.

HOW TO REVIEW ART AS A FEMINIST AND OTHER SPECULATIVE INTENTS

AMY FUNG

We strive to understand ourselves by understanding our past. Place the past in a language that can hold us closer together in the present.

Writing a feminist art review does not make any sense. I have tried and tried again. Art reviews are largely steeped in a capitalist system of power and white male privilege, promoting and propagating its own lineages and legacies. What does the state of art reviewing have to do with feminism? How do you enter a house that was built to exclude you?

I have been thinking about how feminism has been dominated by middle-class and university-educated white women who have fought to be equal to white men instead of standing up for those being oppressed by them.

I have been thinking about the inextricable connection between class conditions and race and gender positions, and how most of my left-leaning peers strive for middle-class comforts.

I have been thinking about the shattered legacies for my generation of queer and feminist artists, writers, and curators, who are still piecing together our histories in the void of HIV/AIDS, in the perpetuation of systematic discriminations, erasing those who came before us.

Thinking is not writing but writing is thinking through the past into a language that is present.

every show looks the same
writhing
in my mouth
should I write it out
in linear notes
for eager readers scanning each line
to see their names
update their CVS
get more shows
so we can do it all again

When I think about my professional lineages, I can only think of texts by women I have never met. I think about articles by Helen Molesworth and Miwon Kwon and I think about living in a place where I could belong. I think about an anecdote from Marcia Tucker's autobiography written in the last years of her life.[1] During the installation of a Marsden Hartley painting as the Whitney's curator of painting and sculpture in the 1970s, she was openly mocked by the installers for her requested adjustments, as either a cunt's hair to the left or a cunt's hair to the right, a scale that is neither metric or imperial, but universal, in making women feel less human.

A feminist is formed through dissent against a system failing. Feminists have disappointed me. Feminists have saved me. Not all women are equal in their inequality. Victorian moralists argued in favor of eugenics in the same breath as for personhood. bell hooks has been saying the exact same thing for over thirty years and we are still hearing her for the first time, every time. That is white supremacist ideology. Working it.

There are lots of people who hate feminists. Enough to hurt them. Kill them. There are also people who hate art reviews. Most of these people are artists. Disdain towards art reviews is a negotiable frustration and this reveals something important in understanding the difference between a feminist and an art reviewer. There is an imbalance of perceptible power between a reviewer and a feminist. The former has perceived power: the gatekeeper. The latter has no power, a redundant obstacle between you and your entitlement. A feminist is so socially degraded that there is no power in identifying as one, no consequences in excluding one. Especially when you have the option to align with Modernists or Minimalists or other Monied white male lineages. People see you better; History treats you kinder.

There is no such thing as apolitical art. Everything is political; the power and privilege to not engage in politics is a position held only by those who can afford to do so.

The actions of history are in and of themselves
compromised,
mediated,
through the rules of language and coded signification.
Language governs and regulates meaning; destroy language and you destroy meaning. To dissent is to render oneself incomprehensible.

A noun is not art,
how you use it is.[2]

Extra-linguistic communication is one way to begin.
Associate alliances touching coalescing
    contagious connections
        beyond linear lines
spreading tangential sprouting
history depleting chronology crumbling into movements
moments influences
disrupting rules of who where when
one may speak.

A regurgitation of power cascading babbling infinitum.
Let feminism be this girl raging at a chandelier.
A miniaturist, a Benedictine, a prisoner.[3]

Re-place absences in your syntax detached. Your omissions of history, art, experiences, endured by women, made under the influence. How we move through this world becomes how we are recording, reflecting, remembering.

A verb is not art,
the way you write through it is.
You can contest this anyway you like. Use your hands and tell me something new.
It doesn't even have to be new, but tell me something.
Anything. Everything.
I don't want to write your criticism anymore. I want nothing to do with your lineages.
I am over it.
I am on the strike that no one is noticing.
I won't compete[4]
Do Less With Less[5]
An ethics of contingency.[6]

A feminist art review could only be a killjoy times a thousand.
I have been thinking about respectability politics in relationship to writing. Professionalism is a form of xenophobia upholding the rules of exclusion. Who are we holding up these standards for and what we are gaining and losing?

We attempt to define feminism as a dynamic state of being, of resisting hierarchal power structures and oppressive systems and ideologies. Art reviews have been more slippery, rooted into a labor of commerce and middle-class meanderings, a neoliberal sinkhole. The politics of aesthetics have nothing to do with either.

To write is to respond
Not posture or promote.
Art reviews may be inherently non-feminist even with the likes of Lucy Lippard and Rosalind Krauss in an old boy's club. To understand the world through only one gender is why Eros is ill.[7] I am ready for more voices reverberating and not echoing:
sharp, shimmer, ignite.

For a speaking subject, the practice of enunciation is a socio-historical embodiment.

Writing making base symbolic markings of an electronic scratch and wink. Connect us across interstices of thoughts, actions, and feelings fueled by an ongoing rage, by the undesirables, by society's most vulnerable. Non-linear legacies are less swayed by power and more through shared ethics. Between the chora and the Internet, non-linearity flourishes. Non-linear communities united form impossible communities, infiltrating each other's nodes of knowledge and desire.

How we write matches what we are going to write.

This is where I am writing from if I am to write at all. How to review art as a feminist is to understand the world and our relative positions within it. How have we come to this position and how will we engage? The limits of language are the limits of knowledge, and we are never outside of language.

This article first appeared as Amy Fung, "How to Review Art as a Feminist and Other Speculative Intents," in *Desire Change: Contemporary Feminist Art in Canada*, ed. by Heather Davis (Montreal: McGill-Queen's University Press with Mentoring Artists for Women's Art, 2017).

1 Marcia Tucker, Chapter 7, "1970–1974," in *A Short Life of Trouble: Forty Years in the New York Art World* (Berkeley: University of California Press, 2008), covering her early years at the Whitney Museum. Tucker went on to found the New Museum before leaving that institution in 1999, trying stand-up comedy and writing her autobiography before passing away at age 66.

2 Julia Kristeva's *Revolution in Poetic Language* (New York: University of Columbia Press, 1984), specifically the chapter "Through the Principles of Language," has informed much of this essay in deciphering that the process of signifying is dialectical to the identification of the subject; poetic language as a signifying practice is generated by a subject within a socio-historical context. When language becomes subject, it means language is held accountable in both a semiotic and symbolic order.

3 Lisa Robertson, *Cinema of the Present* (Toronto: Coach House Books, 2014).

4 "I Won't Compete"—First seen as cross-stitched parade banners by the Feminist Art Gallery (FAG) in Vancouver's Access Gallery, 2013. See also Amber Christensen, Lauren Fournier, and Daniella Sanader's conversation with Deirdre Logue and Allyson Mitchell in this volume, "A Speculative Manifesto for the Feminist Art Fair International."

5 "Do Less With Less"—Limited silkscreen print by the Ladies Invitation Deadbeat Society (LIDS) for the cover and last issue of *FUSE Magazine* (2013).

6 The phrase "an ethics of contingency" is borrowed from a writing workshop led by Cara Benedetto, with gratitude.

7 Gilles Deleuze and Felix Guattari, *A Thousand Plateaus: Capitalism and Schizophrenia* (Minneapolis: University of Minnesota Press, 2007). "Eros Is Ill" is the kernel summary of Deleuze and Guattari's *A Thousand Plateaus.*

MIRA DAYAL: Amy, you published "How to Review Art as a Feminist and other Speculative Intents" in 2017. About halfway through, you state, "I don't want to write your criticism anymore. I am on the strike that no one is noticing." What directly led you to write this, and why did you decide to break that strike, given that you have written criticism since this was published? What terms did you set for yourself in returning to art criticism?

AMY FUNG: That essay was published in 2017, but I wrote it in 2014. It was commissioned for *Desire Change*, the first comprehensive book about feminist art in Canada, a production by Mentoring Artists for Women's Art in Winnipeg. I was asked to write anything I wanted about feminist art in this country. At that point in my life, I had been freelance writing professionally for about twelve years. Full-time freelance writers don't really exist anymore, unless you already have money behind you, but I was doing it in Canada, so I was covering a vast territory, which meant that I was going to and writing about shows I didn't care about, just because they were coming through, or because editors wanted them reviewed. That's how the strike started—I thought, I can't continue to churn out words on shit that I don't care about. When I was asked to write for this book on feminist art,

I was also just finishing a show that I curated with twelve women where I didn't use the words "feminism" or "women." People who visited were like, Wait a minute, these are all women! And I said, Yes, and they're talking about form ... I was really bored with the dialogue. So I wanted to write a poem about breaking language, because language isn't strong enough to hold the ideas that we have. Language comes from a lineage, and lineage is a structure that we all uphold, that we all have to get out of. What if we were speaking from another place?

MD: At what point after that did you decide to start writing about art again?

AF: I was resisting traditional art reviews, and I had not written a traditional review again until recently. I'd started writing in other forms, as art writing. I wrote plays, as art writing. I wrote a book. But I came to a point where a whole generation of artists and writers had forgotten that I could write reviews, and I thought I should see if I still could. So every once in a while, I will write a straight art review, just to prove to myself that I can.

LINDSAY PRESTON ZAPPAS: Are you more selective now about which shows you review?

AF: Absolutely. It's better for everyone.

MD: Ariel, do you want to comment on this? You mentioned that you write more art criticism now, after the publication of your book, than you did before. In some ways, your trajectories are quite different, and both of you also write poetry. What forms of writing do you see as most useful for your objectives as writers, as critics?

ARIEL GOLDBERG: When I've written for glossy art magazines over the past two years, which is new for me, I've felt like an impersonator, or that I'm performing an absurdist exercise. It involves such an intense collaboration with the editor and the tonality of the magazine that it doesn't even feel like my writing at the end. It's just a tool or an experiment. I'm trying to reckon with this question of rage against the canon. What tools are available for interventions? If they're being offered to me, how can I have agendas within them? In terms of what you were saying, Amy, about your communities consisting of people who are engaged in self-interrogation, the form of the mainstream art review is one in which self-interrogation is not just taboo, but not an expectation for what goes into that work. But the lens through which you see the work is the work, arguably. How do we re-create that form in other forms, like in books, where you set the terms?

AF: With straight art criticism, there's a preconceived set of histories and -isms that we all understand, but the critic rarely has an opinion or states an opinion about that history and the problems of those histories; they just talk about where it fits in, if it's any good, and what it looks like. I love reviews and writings that dig in and envelop it within a longer history. And I don't know how you do that without showing your hand. As reviews get shorter and shorter, it's harder and harder to do that. I think that's where art criticism is in a self-imposed crisis.

LPZ: You just described what I really push for in *Carla*—individual perspectives within straight reviews. We've done things like have three writers review the same show, to posit that differing opinions are okay, and to celebrate that. Reviews can come from a traditional, canonical, art historical, or personal perspective. And to go back to audience, who is it for, and what presumed knowledge base do those people have so that they can enter your conversation?

MD: Within books, footnotes can be anchor points that help map the specific communities you're talking about. I actually did read your footnotes, Ariel—I found them to be a helpful resource, something like a syllabus. If you did want to delve deeper into this specific community, even if you're not familiar with it, where would you go? It shows how things are interconnected.

AF: But we can also do that in creative ways, like reading lists.

AUDIENCE: In your book, [Ariel,] you talked about how labeling can also be a way of identifying each other to each other. I think a lot about how you might want to be in the "regular" section of the bookstore, but maybe it's possible to be in the queer section as well—*both*. That's what I want. I want to have my smaller communities because that's important to me, but I want to speak to big communities as well.

AG: I think that's why it doesn't feel satisfying to just propose a new canon, because it's not changing the structure of canonizing, which I think bookstore sections and shelves are manifestations of—they literally spatially structure where books are. At one point when I was writing this book, it was Pride Month, and Strand Bookstore hung huge rainbow flags in the "queer" aisle. They only have a “queer” aisle in June. And it’s weird to see James Baldwin in the queer aisle, because that’s revisionist in a way that’s violent toward the reality of the conditions that Baldwin wrote in. It’s devastating to have to choose to place a book between the queer section and the not-queer section, or every thing else. I want to operate in terms of what I’m bringing into writing, between art and writing, not in this logic of scarcity.

WRITING

LANGUAGE AND VOCABULARY

How can word choices reflect or address the audience of a text or artwork?

What types of institutional or academic vocabularies are worth keeping, and when do they get in the way?

How does a writer's description impact the way an artwork is understood or valued?

How can a writer's language support access, inclusion, and education?

THE LANGUAGES OF ALL-WOMEN EXHIBITIONS

LINDSAY PRESTON ZAPPAS

> "I am still struck by the psychological displacement of women who are alienated by and in language."[1]
> —Lucy R. Lippard

All-women shows have been markedly in vogue in the past few years.[2] Under various curatorial frameworks, these—often-exhaustive—gendered shows always have one thing in common: women. As a woman myself, I often feel sheepish about questioning the structures around these exhibitions as it is well documented that women are underrepresented in the art world, and in need of exposure and support. Still, I bend toward suspicion when galleries and institutions tout an all-women roster. Frustratingly, many of these exhibitions can feel revisionist, or worse, imply a capitalization on the trending socio-political resurgence of women's rights, or the threat to them in our current politics. There are certainly broad problematics within the all-women structure worthy of discussion—the capitalization on the real struggles of women; the masking of uneven gallery rosters that show predominately men; the trend of showing late-career or deceased women artists; the dual demonization and romanticization of motherhood within the biographies of woman artists; and the lack of sustained institutional support for women artists working today. But, I'd like to focus here specifically on the *languages* of all-women exhibitions.

First we must consider how language—in the form of show titles, press releases, promotional materials, and general aura—spawns prejudice before anyone even walks through the front door. Like the joke about vegans: How do you know if an exhibition will include only women? It will tell you. And it often tells you loudly, and in advance. In a 2016 *Atlantic* article, Sarah Boxer described visiting "Women of Abstract Expressionism" at the Denver Art Museum: "I could see banners announcing the women's exhibition from a distance. WOMEN WOMEN WOMEN. It almost looked like they were announcing a strip tease." As Boxer walked closer, a minuscule text that read, "Women of Abstract Expressionism" could be seen in small type, low on the banner. Boxer also recalls the cover for the catalogue of "WACK! Art and the Feminist Revolution"—the massive all-women exhibition at MOCA in 2007—which features Martha Rosler's clippings of naked women from *Playboy,* "as if to announce, 'sexy ladies inside!'"[3] While the Rosler work was exhibited in "WACK!," *choosing* that particular work for the catalogue image problematically gave primacy to the fetishization of the nude female, if even while being subversive.

The 2017 exhibition "CUNT" at Venus Over Los Angeles chose a more subtle promotional tack, its title notwithstanding: a square baby-pink poster with the exhibition title centered, all caps, in white. While understated, the graphic recalls normative baby-girl colors as well as the anatomy of female genitalia. While the exhibition featured fantastic work, that poster (and the brashness of the word *cunt*) infected any pure experience of the work apart from its association to female genitalia. There are certainly many convincing arguments towards reclaiming and normalizing the word *cunt*[4]—even students in early feminist programs were instructed to repeat the word *cunt* until it was removed of its derogatory associations.[5] Still, utilizing it as a moniker for a group show by women shrouds the work included under the complicated social and linguistic baggage that the word carries.

In the "WACK!" catalogue, Eva Hesse's incomparable work *Hang Up* (1966) is organized under the heading "Gendered Space" though historically this work has been associated with minimalism, not feminism. This reframing of context recalls the way in which Ana Mendieta's work has been adopted by various feminist groups and causes over the years, while Mendieta herself was "dissatisfied with being reduced to one vision of feminism, or one articulation of identity."[6] For instance, white feminist groups looped her work in with the representation of The Goddess, "a trendy subtopic" of the era, although Mendieta's relationship to goddesses was more "complex and volatile."[7] Her work was also contextualized within restricting feminist dialogues of the body, victimhood, and violence. This type of singularity was precisely what Mendieta's work was meant to reject, and these misrepresentations ultimately led to her resignation from the feminist group A.I.R. in 1982.[8] Charles Merewether explains, "the question of naming has afflicted the scholarship and reception of Ana Medieta's work."[9] It is indeed this question of naming that is paramount in the re-historicization of women artists today, as it shapes the future narrative of their historically tenuous careers.

Often all-women exhibitions include the qualifier, *woman*, almost as a sort of warning of what can be expected of the work. In researching this article, I reached out to Micol Hebron, who has been actively tracking gender inequality on gallery rosters since 2013. "I think the more complicated and perhaps insidious reason that this is a problem is the longstanding inherent bias against women's work," Hebron wrote to me in a recent email. "Women's labor(s) are historically valued less: their wages are lower, their art sells for less, and the aesthetics associated with 'women's work' are considered less cool. So, an all-women show can be seen as a concession of sorts."

When curators and gallerists preface exhibitions with an admission of the artist's gender, it makes the fact impossible to ignore and surely has an effect on the way in which the artist's work is being viewed. A wonderful exhibition at the Landing gallery last summer, which included stunning works by Tanya Aguiñiga, Loie Hollowell, and Lenore Tawney, was titled dryly—and reductively—"3 Women." The title was lifted from a 1977 Robert Altman film, yet, dropped on this context of three intergenerational artists, it became a descriptor, a confession. Under this titling, the indomitable weavings of Tawney, who worked alongside Agnes Martin and Ellsworth Kelly in the 60s, seemed to sink into categories of "women's work," while Hollowell's expansive and intricate paintings read more explicitly like pretty little vaginas.

We never hear an exhibition described as an all-men exhibition, since it is the understood normal. As such, as we constantly denote *woman*, we are reinforcing men as the engrained default. In her introduction to *The Pink Glass Swan,* the feminist art critic Lucy Lippard describes working on her own writing and constantly referring to "the critic" as *he*, "as though my own identity and actions had been subsumed by patriarchal nomenclature."[10]

As we incessantly insert women back into art history, we in turn agree with the normative patriarchal telling of history that tells us that these women need inserting—while, as Griselda Pollock insisted, "feminist history began inside art history."[11] As we continue to group women together in exhibitions, and insist on qualifying the exhibition as belonging to women, we keep women on the outside of mainstream art. As my editor Aaron Horst commented in a recent conversation, "it makes the fact of being a woman *and* an artist somehow remarkable." Famously, when asked at a party "what women artists think," Joan Mitchell turned to Elaine De Kooning, exclaiming, "Elaine, let's get the hell out of here."[12]

Perhaps to combat these musty normatives of art history, curators of all-women exhibitions slap on language that *opposes* weakness: *power, revolution, radical, escape, get the fuck out, wack!* This combativeness often feels put on, as if we must insist and argue that women might be able to wield power. Though not specifically an all-women exhibition, in reference to the titling of "Trigger: Gender as a Tool and a Weapon" (a 2017–18 group exhibition of mostly LGBTQ-identified artists at the New Museum), Peter Schjeldahl wrote, "the four nouns in the title of the [show] go off like improvised explosive devices, boding civil strife." A beat later, Schjeldahl concedes that the works in the exhibition don't live up to its corralling and boosterish nomenclature. "The show's provocative title turns out to function rather like the old vaudeville pistol that emits a little flag imprinted 'BANG.'"[13] This sort of blanket, categorical re-contextualization that the exhibition titling imbues is precisely problematic as it limits—or makes difficult—a reading of the artwork under any other conceptual framework.

In reference to the titling of "SOGTFO (Sculpture or Get the Fuck Out)," a five-woman sculpture exhibition at Ghebaly Gallery, Jonathan Griffin wrote, "Even subverted, its aggressive tone seems unfitting for the general measured output of these five artists. None are polemical about their gender, and it's hard to imagine any of them coming up with a title as caustic as 'SOGTFO'—which, of course, they didn't."[14] While it is potentially the case that women artists are consulted and collaborated with in the development of exhibition titles (as in fact was the case with "CUNT"[15]), elsewhere the titling is meant to evoke struggle and combat that isn't inherit in the work itself. In the case of titling "WACK!," Connie Butler explains that "the exclamatory title of the exhibition is intended to recall the bold idealism that characterized the feminist movement during [the late 60s and 70s]... The violent and sexual connotations of *WACK* serve to reinforce feminism's affront to the patriarchal system."[16] These abrasive nomenclatures seem to perpetuate the stereotype of the brash and wild feminist, while also reeking of self-congratulatory prose, suggesting that the institution who undoubtedly titled said exhibition has rediscovered—and tamed?—a wild bunch of feminists.

Yet, to a large extent, many women in these monstrous exhibitions do not consider their work feminist at all (and some decline participation). It is an arduous task to clarify the difference between a feminist framework and actual feminist art,[17] and the all-women context "allow[s] for some form of erasure or fitting women into existing parameters."[18]

The way in which we are speaking, writing, and naming all-women exhibitions seems paramount to the ways in which the next generation will understand the contributions of women artists. As Helen Molesworth has said, "the only way to get diversity is to actually do it."[19] It is this *doing* that can get complicated as institutions constantly point to diversity they are implementing—*look Ma, no hands!*—with promotional language and curatorial strategies. Language instills pattern; pattern becomes habit. "The habits of mind that our culture has instilled in us from infancy shape our orientation to the world and our emotional responses to the objects we encounter," wrote Guy Deutscher in a *New York Times* article about how language shapes reality. "They may also have a marked impact on our beliefs, values and ideologies."[20] As such, all-women exhibitions may have the power to accelerate or neuter efforts towards the equalization of gender biases in the arts. And much of this power comes down to the naming; the language that garnishes press releases and show cards may in fact be reinforcing our ingrained biases rather than liberating us from them.

This article first appeared as Lindsay Preston Zappas, "The Languages of All-Women Exhibitions," *Carla*, October 25, 2017, https://contemporaryartreview.la/the-languages-of-all-women-exhibitions/.

1 Lucy Lippard, "Introduction: Moving Targets/Concentric Circles: Notes from the Radical Whirlwind," *The Pink Glass Swan: Selected Feminist Essays on Art* (New York: New Press, 1995).

2 "Revolution in the Making: Abstract Sculpture by Women, 1947–2016" at Hauser & Wirth, "Escape Attempts" at Shulamit Nazrian, "SOGTFO" at Ghebaly Gallery, "Power" at Sprüth Magers, "Signifying Form" at the Landing, "CUNT" at Venus Over Los Angeles, "Radical Women: Latin American Art, 1960–1985" at the Hammer, and "We Wanted a Revolution: Black Radical Women, 1965–85" at The California African American Museum come to mind as notable examples in Los Angeles from 2015 to 2017.

3 Sarah Boxer, "An Era for Women Artists?," *The Atlantic*, December 2016.

4 The etymology of the word *cunt* relates to the celebration of the feminine and the goddess, where its sister word, *vagina*, has more violent and aggressive root word connotations, translating to sheath or scabbard in which to thrust a sword. Gillian Schutte, "C Is for Cunt," *Ms. Magazine* (blog), November 27, 2012, http://msmagazine.com/blog/2012/11/27/c-is-for-cunt/.

5 Mira Schor, "The Ism That Dare Not Speak Its Name," in *A Decade of Negative Thinking* (Durham: Duke University Press, 2009), 30.

6 Julia Bryan-Wilson, "Against the Body: Interpreting Ana Mendieta," *Ana Medieta: Traces* (London: Hayward Publishing, 2013), 35.

7 Ibid., 31.

8 Ibid., 134–135.

9 Charles Merewether, "From Inception to Dissolution: An Essay on Expenditure in the work of Ana Medieta," *Ana Mendieta* (Barcelona: Poligrapha, 1998), 148.

10 Lippard, *The Pink Glass Swan*, 13.

11 Griselda Pollock, "Feminist Interventions in Art's Histories," *Kritische Berichte* 16, no. 1 (1998).

12 Boxer.

13 Peter Schjeldahl, "Safe Space: A Show on Gender Soothes More Than It Unsettles," *The New Yorker*, October 9, 2017.

14 Jonathan Griffin, "SOGTFO at François Ghebaly," *Carla*, issue 1, April 2015.

15 *Carla Podcast*, Episode 1, October 2017, https://contemporaryartreview.la/episode-1/.

16 Cornelia Butler, "Art and Feminism: An Ideology of Shifting Criteria," *WACK! Art and the Feminist Revolution* (Los Angeles: Museum of Contemporary Art, 2007), 15.

17 Cecilia Fajardo-Hill, "The Invisibility of Latin American Women Artists: Problematizing Art Historical and Curatorial Practices," in *Radical Women: Latin American Art, 1960–1985* (New York: Prestel, 2017), 23–24.

18 Ibid., 21.

19 Boxer.

20 Guy Deitsher, "Does Your Language Shape How You Think?," *New York Times Magazine*, August 26, 2010.

SIMPLICITY CRAVING
ARIEL GOLDBERG

> There was a dyke story in one of Max's porn magazines. It was my favorite, but not because I liked it exactly. Reading it by the light of my flashlight was like examining a photograph of dead relatives.
> —Camille Roy[1]

> Help us poison position.
> —Dawn Lundy Martin[2]

I got a speeding ticket from a surveillance camera on my way to what was being talked about as the biggest and most controversial show featuring artists who represented homosexuality. Half a year later, my father handed me a blurry photo he got in the mail with his car's license plate and the amount due. I am willing to confess I harbored a strange enthusiasm for "Hide/Seek: Difference and Desire in American Portraiture." I thought it would be an easy target to exercise the nascent argument of this essay—"it's dangerous to label art queer." The show was curated by Jonathan D. Katz and David C. Ward, two white gay men, and presented an overwhelming majority of gay male artists and subjects. In 2010, "Hide/Seek" was not "new" or historic outside its tenuous government walls and focus on portraiture. It was record-breaking only in terms of how many tax dollars funded it.[3]

The show compelled me to ramble through recent histories on my own, not only by way of the curators. Through interlibrary loan I ordered the catalogue "Extended Sensibilities: Homosexual Presence in Contemporary Art," the New Museum's now trendy sounding 1982 show. Some artists refused to be a part of this show; they refused to be thematized, or to be outed. Then I read the catalogue for the 1995 Berkeley Art Museum/Pacific Film Archive's "In a Different Light," which announced itself as the "first queer art show" that included artists who did not necessarily identify as queer, but the curators interpreted their work as queer. Robert Atkins reflects on how "In a Different Light" "rejected the notion of identity politics in favor of an amorphous notion of queer sensibility."[4]

To include artists and writers who didn't identify as queer was a decision that appeared to Atkins "apolitical" and "over-aestheticized." A lukewarm form of irrelevance characterized the "Hide/Seek" show in its adherence to a flawed canon. Yet this canon still exuded risk within the context of the National Portrait Gallery. Many arts organizations across the country responded in protest to the Smithsonian Institution's baffling decision to censor David Wojnarowicz's *A Fire in My Belly* (1986–87) from "Hide/Seek," of which I saw an "emergency screening" at San Francisco Camerawork, directly after the work was removed from the show.[5]

I had visited SF Camerawork a handful of times already in fall 2010 to see the exhibit "Suggestions of a Life Being Lived," which represents the more common "queer art" show, one at a small nonprofit in a city with no shortage of gay and queer culture. I was eager to see a show that, as the press release promised, was "unconcerned with coming-out narratives." In contrast to the looming 1995 precedent of the organizational structure of "In a Different Light," the curators, Danny Orendorff and Adrienne Skye Roberts, wanted to address "how a sense of liberated queerness is pursued and mediated within public spaces and behaviors."[6]

Gay Shame protest documentation and Killer Banshee ephemera hung in the entrance to the gallery; records of direct action activism served as the entry point of the show. Adrienne gave me a guided tour of the exhibition as I interviewed her. I held on to her catchphrase: "What I'm interested in is a queer set of political alliances." I was admittedly flirting a little with Adrienne, and hoping to impress her with my handheld tape recorder. She had mentioned a partner, but I wondered if that also meant an open relationship. When I asked her why, on encountering this show, I felt so frustrated with the phrase "queer art," she told me she could relate. She had just been interviewed for the web series Culture Wire, where Meg Shiffler of the San Francisco Arts Commission asked, "What's the show about? What is queer photography?" Adrienne responded: "I don't know. I have a better sense of what queer means to me. Queer art is what makes that sense of queerness visible."[7]

Shiffler's proposition to define something hit as the gravest offense. When wall texts, press releases, and artist statements are littered with the word "queer," I start to grow suspicious of what the word is trying to say, as if temporarily fooled into the word functioning as a measuring tool. The word "queer" easily loses its gunpowder when used effusively. In what ways can language persist as "radical" when the language is being used in a predictable routine? My primary apprehension about "Suggestions of a Life Being Lived" was based on the concern that this was the one chance a San Francisco alternative art space gets at a "queer" show, outside the month of June, when there are always multiple "queer art" shows. What did I want from this show? For there to be art with no trace of stereotypical "queerness"? That stereotype is both too wide and too subjective to understand. Knee-jerk associations with queerness are often what shows like "Suggestions" are working to resist. I had to shake that feeling that there wasn't enough space for artists who are queer. A catalogue for "Suggestions" went to print after the exhibition so that the curators could include their evolving thoughts on the work they'd curated. They reflect on the process of making the exhibit in the contemporary climate of assimilation and violence. Adrienne describes how the illusion of "police officers escorting [gay pride parades] rather than raiding our bars ... completely denies the reality that there still exists state-sanctioned violence against minority subjects, including queer people, in our cities, on the streets, and through the prison system."[8] Halfway through their conversation, which spans the entire length of the catalogue, Adrienne says to Danny, "I think we should also talk about our ambivalence towards the category 'queer art.'"[9]

I have found this ambivalence toward the category to be its most common characteristic. When I first saw "Suggestions," I crudely tried to put the work on a spectrum of "queer content" to imagine if a curator of a "queer art show" ever evaluated how much "queerness" was in a work. The show was organized around themes such as the public sphere, intentional communities, utopia, and self-determination. Kirstyn Russell's large-scale photos of landscapes are whispers of "queer content." Her photo series *Where We Are Not Known* features gay bars or building exteriors with traces of a word that can be read as queer, even if only by the recontextualizing frame of the camera. The "Dyke" on signage for a store shows a fraction of a business owner's last name. I imagine how people may watch Russell when she is constructing or finding gay signposts, how that live action of cropping is a quiet but powerful performance. The viewers in the gallery, when looking at the pictures framed on the wall, stand removed from the scene. But postcards of the images, on a rack free for the taking, are ready to travel outside the gallery. Aay Preston-Myint represents a seemingly louder version of "queer content" with *SMILE II*, a photo booth installation that "invites visitors to imagine themselves within a post-apocalyptic family portrait studio where gender and sexuality have become fluid." Crocheted beards, wigs, and other textile costumes made by Preston-Myint reroute gender norms to riff on the conformity underlying the portrait studio. As opposed to Russell's finished photos, visitors must ultimately produce Preston-Myint's work at the site of the gallery.

The failed endeavor of quantifying queerness calls on the verb capability of "queer" as a lifeline to escape the fixity of an adjective. At least verbs need action to be performed. I have watched the unsavory trends of the art market temporarily crown ever-incomplete versions of "the political" or "the queer" as fashionable. In order for "queer" or "political" to also be risky adjectives, they must fall out of fashion. One cannot control all the language that swarms around art. Especially unrealistic is the possibility of control over which word form (adjective versus verb) is used. I am reminded of the game rock, paper, scissors. An adjective is the paper that covers the rock, suffocating it, a verb the scissors splitting the paper into a new shape. I hope the demarcation of work that critiques hegemonic discourse is not the only work named "political." I like to use the word political to describe work that isn't "counter-whatever-the-culture-is" but hides its opinions—if the art has any at all—and maneuvers to mirror the safety of the status quo.

"Suggestions of a Life Being Lived" does not use the word "queer" or "gay" in the title, nor does "Hide/Seek: Difference and Desire in American Portraiture." I cannot parse the words "difference" and "desire" as euphemism or rejection. Many of the smaller-scale group shows that thematize queerness play effusively with the word queer. For example, San Francisco's SOMArts June 2011 show was named "Queer It Yourself—Tools for Survival." But "Hide/Seek" did not serve an explicit queer community. More than one friend told me that they saw the show with their parents. The national exhibition brought a discussion to supposedly not "queer" or "gay" spaces or relationships. This gesture to produce "culture" felt dizzying because the national government's dominant culture has been to keep artists who are gay or queer without funding—in other words, to keep artists who are gay or queer as unseen as possible, which ultimately has threatened the most basic survival of artists who are gay or queer, especially those without independent wealth or patrons.

"Hide/Seek" could afford to produce a perfect-bound catalogue that, in its girth, resembles the level in Super Mario Brothers when everything is enlarged. Long after the guards gently reminded me the National Portrait Gallery was closing, I studied the show's every decision about how to present information. I was torn between learning new things and feeling frustrated by the curators' blind spots. The wall text, reproduced to face all the plates in the "Hide/Seek" catalogue, is concerned with decoding the "desire" embedded in the portraits by pointing out that either the artist was known to be gay/queer or the subject was gay/queer. Katz and Ward's quantification was that simple, which I find devastating. Berenice Abbott, whose portrait of Janet Flanner adorns the "Hide/Seek" catalogue cover, once responded to questions about her homosexuality with the statement, "I am a photographer, not a lesbian."[10] Abbott vociferously denied "homosexual" framing of both her life and her wide-ranging body of work, which includes New York City in its constant state of transformation, physics textbook illustrations, and portraits of artists and writers in 1920s Paris. Her early portraiture documents what history now refers to as a formidable cadre of lesbians, though Abbott and her contemporaries did not call themselves that.

The image in "Hide/Seek" that continues to haunt me is Peter Hujar's portrait of Susan Sontag. The wall text reads: "[Sontag] later regretted that she had not spoken more publicly about her lesbianism, but that kind of personal revelation was at odds to her cool analytical tendency."[11] In Hujar's portrait, she is on her back, glancing upward over her shoulder, supremely self-satisfied. Her chest appears almost flat in a ribbed turtleneck. Drips of hardened white paint are visible on the imperfect wall behind her. When writing about this image from memory, I saw endless drafts of paper with messy handwriting strewn about her like a fan, which is actually a photo Annie Leibovitz took of Sontag but I saw it as a double exposure onto Hujar's portrait. In 2012, Sunita and I made it off the waitlist to see the Builders Association's premiere of *Sontag: Reborn*, her adapted journals. A video of an older Sontag plays throughout, talking back to the younger Sontag. Moe Angelos, who has been working as an out lesbian in downtown New York theater since the early 80s, plays Sontag at both ages. The adaptation highlights the entries where Sontag struggled painfully with lovers, soaked up philosophy, wandered helplessly as a prodigy in Europe, and whoops, got married. Having just read the first published journal in the trilogy, I mouthed along to the line I had transcribed into my journal: "My desire to write is connected with my homosexuality. I need the identity as a weapon, to match the weapon that society has against me."[12] I left the play unsure of how to maintain my criticism of Sontag's not being out enough and of the historical dishonesty of the "Hide/Seek" exhibit's focus on the fulcrum of out versus not out. I started to understand how Sontag came of age in a different time, a time when the word "queer" wasn't actively used as a label to describe a potential aesthetic, a time when she coded a related endeavor with the word "camp."

Sontag's journals send me to an uncomfortable memory of seeing Leibovitz's retrospective at the Brooklyn

Museum in 2007. Looking at the many pictures of Sontag felt like I'd suddenly found a yellowing lesbian newsletter past its heyday of circulation. Sontag is pictured in bed, in a bath, in the hospital, on vacation. Leibovitz also shot still lifes of Sontag's literary traces, such as an early Apple computer alight with a chapter to her book *The Volcano Lover* (1992). Standing in the galleries, facing the photos on the wall, I learned for the first time that Sontag was staring into Leibovitz's camera as her lover. I strained to remember my photography history classroom, the lights turned off, where a slide projector hummed next to my guide, Shelley Rice, who thrives on adding brassy gossip to her memorized lectures. I couldn't recall if Shelley digressed into a story about Sontag and Leibovitz. It was much easier for me to associate the slides of Claude Cahun's self-portraits with lesbian history than Sontag's *On Photography*.

I reread Sontag's *New York Times* obituary, which clearly maps her marriage to a man, and their divorce, which, in the scheme of her life, was a blip. In the year of her death, 2004, the *Times* mentioned absolutely nothing about her lesbian partnership. Only an insulting trace: "She was photographed by Annie Leibovitz for an Absolut Vodka ad." *The Believer* ran an article on how divisive the international-straight-mainstream-media's obituaries were for Sontag: the overtly supportive and then the overtly undermining of her writing and thinking.[13] One point remained united in these obituaries: no mention of her dykehood. I think of AA Bronson, thirteen years Sontag's junior. Bronson's career as a successful gay male artist is credible in the art world. He is a sort of inspiration to mostly young gay male-identified artists, while Sontag is a problem for me to reckon with.

Now that Sontag is dead, her lesbian relationships seem to be all people want to talk about. When Sontag writes, "Being queer makes me feel more vulnerable,"[14] she takes on both the "strange" and the "slur" of the word "queer"'s official definitions. "Queer" sounds quaint in the context of her journals, but Sontag's irresolute relationship with her sexuality and its relationship to her work is far from outdated. I imagine her handwriting as I read her mass-produced journals, the typeset words working like a stencil to help me draw a line between Sontag's choice not to "come out" and the zero pressure I feel to be silent about my sexuality. Sontag's rock-star intellectual status complicates her desire for privacy. Which begs the obvious question: Would she have had so many book contracts with mainstream publishers if she had been "out"?

I had a dream that Sarah Schulman attempted to clarify how lesbian poet Kay Ryan's absence of lesbian content is as predictable as a clock's second hand. Time is upside down. Minutes don't add up. Things are moving slowly like gravity nodding its head no. I said what about Eileen Myles's aesthetic of complete straightforwardness, where the "lesbian" cannot exactly be excised? Schulman demanded eye contact; look at me, "I have been censored because I say what no one wants to hear." I tried to reply, "But it's also how you say it." In the dream, Schulman's voice grew soft after this gust of polemic. "All I really want are for my lesbian protagonists to be with all the other protagonists." I then dreamt of going to my playground of a bookstore and finding the "LGBT section" (or "queer section") gone, and Schulman's books shelved in "fiction" and "nonfiction." I panicked. I wanted the section back. I woke up and thought of the Bureau of General Services, with its separate shelves for all the various identity and genre based subdivisions a queer bookstore houses, like neighbors who may or may not say hi to each other.

Then I was actually scouring a used bookstore in Lincoln, Nebraska—looking for books to help me write this essay that became a chapter of *The Estrangement Principle*—

on a stop along the cross-country drive that pulled me back to New York. I asked the bookseller to point me to the LGBT section, which was tucked away in the back, a cove akin to the porn section of a video store. I found Schulman's *My American History: Lesbian and Gay Life During the Reagan and Bush Years* (1994) on a stack yet to be alphabetized and shelved. Then I walked across to the poetry section and found a few of Kay Ryan's books. I told Jocelyn Saidenberg about this problem as we sat in the packed audience of a screening for *T'Ain't Nobody's Bizness: Queer Blues Divas of the 1920s*.[15] Jocelyn asked: "Can't we have both?" Ryan and Schulman's books should be located in "both" sections. Jocelyn was one of the first people to answer my awkward call for interviews about how art is labeled "queer." She invited me over for dinner in her amazingly adult home. I remember cabinets encasing books, to reduce dust and enhance archival endurance. Jocelyn served me a nourishing vegetable curry while I asked her to tell me about how she came to be a poet in San Francisco. I didn't turn on my tape recorder. I left the conversation understanding how queerness is extremely valuable because she told me about the ways her queerness has been honored, not marginalized.

Jocelyn's life as a poet, she told me, is really a lot about friendship. I began to understand "queerness" in poetry functioning similarly to the ways friendship unfolds in the life of the writer. At the early stages of writing *The Estrangement Principle*, I read Jocelyn's work fervently because I identified with it. Like my bad experiment to quantify the "queerness" of the art in the "Suggestions of a Life Being Lived" exhibition, I started to study Jocelyn's poetry by locating the "queer" content as though tracing a map. I was massaging the question of, am I trying to theorize the untheorizable? Jocelyn traverses a range that includes lesbian subjectivity in the first person as well as challenging the gender binary altogether. Jocelyn begins her first book, *Mortal City*, by addressing the process of resisting the impulse to name something:

> this is called
> the impermanence of things
> of nothing shows
> behind the image
> except the nail
> and the wall[16]

Artistic production is a routine and so Jocelyn's poem shows us the image's backside. In asking how visual representations operate in codes, the narrator turns their attention to the structural support underneath "the image." In the contractual poem entitled "SIGN HERE," Jocelyn instructs the reader to "desert the surface" and "wrestle platitudes."

Jocelyn's context is the fairly insular world of Bay Area experimental poetry. She has published with small presses, which operate with a different type of visibility than Kay Ryan's publisher, Grove Press, does. This is a crude division and one based on the numeric quantifiers: book sales and distribution, grants and awards. I was interested in Jocelyn's work because she accepted my invitation to ask her about how and why she wrote it. I am always reckoning with the reality that poets are rarely household names in this country and that the relative notion of a queer's invisibility is not so different than a poet's invisibility. For a person who is queer and a poet (among many other "things") their potential "invisibility" becomes a long division equation with a trail of numbers stretching past the decimal point. By invisibility, I do not mean to make visibility the goal; I'm invested more in "invisibility" as an honorable un-doing of the popularity routine. "Visibility" with a capital V often prioritizes the lowest common denominator of the masses as opposed to prioritizing the material needs of a poet who is queer.

These investigations of "queer art" have been a cover for what feels like many urgent and messy conversations. When I began writing, I was desperate to feel swaddled in dyke mentorship. But I never admitted that to myself, exactly. Instead, I did things like get Judith Butler's haircut. The questioning of labeling is so firmly planted in history, yet the reappearance of the question isn't exactly redundant. It's like tourists going through the motion of taking the same picture of a beautiful site. Everyone needs their own copy. Why did I pretend, with the flimsiness of a haircut, to look like Judith Butler? I criticize myself now for choosing a famous philosopher to be in imagined dialogue with. She's packaged as a hero, ready to be adored by the newly queer. Why did I study Jocelyn's writing? Why did I parse Sontag's obituaries? I think about the bizarre façade in ethnic longing. So what if I am drawn to these white Jewish lesbians of varying generations away from mine? There was a moment when talking to Jocelyn and reading her work helped me fit some pieces into place: the legibility of art labeled as queer depends on highly specific localized groups of people and the individuals supporting each other within these communities. "Queer" means little when stripped from its context. There was a moment when I was trying to reach Kay Ryan through her agent and eventually gave up. I had to remind myself I'm not searching for long-lost family—I'm trying to build my own.

Perhaps it is not that I want to stop critiquing what is called "queer art" but just to recover from being barraged by it. My eyes grow tired when any word repeats. I lose interest. I don't want reinvention. I want more specific language. This particular naming needs a counterpart of always asking about all the art that falls outside the "queer" category that might really be sharing something with this category. When I began writing *The Estrangement Principle*, a friend warned me about how I was using the word "scene," not "community," in my understanding of social and artistic landscapes. I asked, "What's the difference?" not yet understanding how cynical and critical the word "scene" sounded. Like I was locked out. But really, I was young(er) and hadn't been in one place long enough to contribute to various communities built around shared interests and experiences. I could only have been compelled to write about this tenuous sense of belonging at that acute moment of estrangement.

1 Camille Roy, *The Rosy Medallions* (Berkeley: Kelsey Street Press, 1995), 27.

2 Dawn Lundy Martin, *The Morning Hour* (New York: The Poetry Society of America, 2003), 8.

3 Holland Cotter, "Sexuality in Modernism: The (Partial) History," *The New York Times*, December 10, 2010. Cotter writes, "The whole enterprise looked like an exercise in Hall of Fame-building, rather than like an effort to chip away at the very idea of hierarchy and exclusion."

4 Robert Atkins, "Goodbye Lesbian/Gay History, Hello 'Queer Sensibility': Meditating on Curatorial Practice," *College Art Association Journal* 55, no. 4 (1996): 80–85. Atkins criticizes curators Lawrence Rinder and Nayland Blake of the Berkeley Art Museum's 1996 "In a Different Light," as well as *Art in America*'s "After Stonewall," which was a "package of 12 interviews [that] was conceived and realized by Holland Cotter... At its most problem-atic, the contemporary-oral-history format obviates any give and take. This reader yearned, for instance, for Cotter's response to Hugh Steer's observation that 'gay art is a marketing label... it's important to discuss it and expose the fallacy of lumping us all together.'"

5 Chuck Mobley, Julia Haas, Alison Maurer, Irene Gustafson, Jonathan D. Katz, Kim Anno, Julian Carter, and Robert Atkins, "Emergency Screening: *A Fire in My Belly*—a Short Film by David Wojnarowicz and Panel Discussion," SF Camerawork, December 10, 2010.

6 "Suggestions of a Life Being Lived," SF Camerawork, San Francisco, CA, September 9–October 23, 2010. The exhibition featured Steven Miller, Tara Mateik, Killer Banshee, Gay Shame, Kirstyn Russell, Jeannie Simms, Lenn Keller, Mercury Vapor Studios, Chris Vargas, Greg Youmans, Jason Fritz Michael, Aay Preston-Myint, Allyson Mitchell, Eric Stanley, Torsten Zenas Burns, and Darrin Martin.

7 Adrienne Skye Roberts, in discussion with the author, October 13, 2010.

8 *Suggestions of a Life Being Lived*, ed. Danny Orendorff and Adrienne Skye Roberts (San Francisco: SF Camerawork, 2011), 13.

9 Ibid., 34.

10 Jonathan D. Katz, *Hide/Seek: Difference and Desire in American Portraiture* (Washington, DC: Smithsonian Books, 2011), 23. Katz quoting Abbott in an interview with Kaucyila Brooke. Katz also cites Tee A. Corinne's self-published 1996 book *The Lesbian Eye of Berenice Abbott*.

11 Peter Hujar, "Susan Sontag," "Hide/Seek: Difference and Desire in American Portraiture" (Washington DC: National Portrait Gallery), 2010, museum exhibition label.

12 Susan Sontag, *Reborn: Journals and Notebooks, 1947–1963*, ed. David Rieff (New York: Farrar, Straus and Giroux, 2008), 221.

13 Lisa Levy, "Critical Intimacy: Comparing the Paradoxical Obituaries of Susan Sontag," *The Believer*, April 2006. Terry Castle eulogized Sontag in a very "out" way by reflecting on difficulty in their friendship in *The London Review of Books* in 2005. Castle also cites Allan Gurganus's *The Advocate* obituary, which expresses the wish that Sontag came out.

14 Sontag, *Reborn*, 221.

15 *T'Aint Nobody's Bizness: Queer Blues Divas of the 1920s*, dir. Robert Philipson (San Francisco: Shoga Films Foundation, 2013).

16 Saidenberg, *Mortal City* (San Diego: Parenthesis Writing Series, 1998), 7.

MIRA DAYAL: Ariel, "Simplicity Craving" is the third chapter of your book *The Estrangement Principle*, in which you discuss your task of tracking the term "queer art," which you write is overused and predictable and not always desired by the artist (or artwork) that it is intended to describe. You open this chapter by stating that the nascent argument of the book was, "It's dangerous to label art queer." But by the end of the chapter, your thesis has shifted: "Perhaps it is not that I want to stop critiquing what is called 'queer art' but just to recover from being barraged by it .... I don't want reinvention. I want more specific language." Since or while writing that book, how have you attempted to find more specific language? I want to link this question to your statement that "the legibility of art labeled as queer depends on highly specific, localized groups of people and the individuals supporting each other within these communities." Can you talk more about your ideas on the relations between language and community and how you've tried to address that in your own writing?

ARIEL GOLDBERG: I wrote a book troubling the labeling of art as "queer" with a lot of different agendas. I'm glad I wrote about the tension, the resistance I felt toward seeing the word "queer" next to "art." It wasn't producing meaning for me, and I tried to understand why. It felt so contingent on other factors, like who was doing the naming. I started writing this book in 2010 in the San Francisco Bay area, so the context is really different. I was 27, I think, when I started writing, and I was new to the concept of different artistic and literary communities. The book is about questioning the label and feeling unsatisfied with the label because so much falls outside of it. Why use this one identity label and not other ones, for example?

But the book is more of a journey toward figuring out how I want to build relationships with other writers and artists that then become "communities." That's the shadow project of the book. It begins with questioning why a book is called "gay literature" on the cover—literally talking about surfaces. What do the codes of choices of blurb writers mean? What does it mean if Eileen Myles blurbs a book? That's one of the questions I ask in the first chapter. By the third chapter, I'm relenting and saying, I'm surrounded by this and I've become inured to this question of what queer art is or why things are called queer art. I think I just wanted to, as Amy was saying, reinvent language or escape language, rattle the tools that were given. I have stopped caring about the label "queer art." It was a temporal experience that faded. I don't feel the unrest anymore, and in fact when I wrote this book, I did not identify as an art critic or a literary critic. I was just out of an MFA program in creative writing, trying to understand myself in relation to other histories of creative production. Since I wrote the book, I have been tasked with art criticism. When trying to write in so many words, I've realized that saying, "Art made by queer people," or, "Art called queer," is grammatically awkward and takes up more words than saying, "queer art." That language I was trying to understand—it's just shorter. That's why it's in the press release. And I've started calling things queer. I'm not immune. It is easier, in certain ways. But what gets lost in that facility?

AMY FUNG: The meaning of "queer" changes as well. In terms of this question that you ask in your book, Why am I on this shelf and not on that shelf?, so much of it is marketing, right? It's not always the writer's decision; it's the publisher's. What does it mean to have a gay poet blurb your book? Will they want to? Why are you asking them? That goes back to lineage as well, right? Can it be a negative thing? Is that coded or is that wanting to use the power that they have? I ask because Eileen blurbed my book.... I asked them to blurb it because I respect them as a writer.

AG: And, unfortunately, the contemporary climate is one in which we're more used to and suspicious of identities being instrumentalized by institutions or by publishers. How do we escape that and go back to more basic ideas of seeing oneself in a lineage or making an homage or intergenerational connection?

LINDSAY PRESTON ZAPPAS: I loved the part of your essay where you talked about queer as a noun and queer as an adjective ...

MD: This is toward the beginning of the chapter: "In order for 'queer' or 'political' to also be risky adjectives, they must fall out of fashion. One cannot control all the language that storms around art. Especially unrealistic is the possibility of control over which word form—adjective or verb—is used. I am reminded of the game rock, paper, scissors. An adjective is the paper that covers the rock, suffocating it. A verb is scissors splitting the paper into a new shape. I hope the demarcation of work that critiques hegemonic discourse is not the only work named 'political.' I like to use the word 'political' to describe work that isn't counter-whatever-the-culture-is but rather hides its opinions, if the art has any at all, and maneuvers to mirror the safety of the status quo." That analogy conveys how the forms of this word can battle each other or jockey for priority.

LPZ: And they can adapt to different usages in different contexts. One might have more power and the other might stifle or cover it. A lot of what I was talking about in my essay, too, was about the word "woman," the adjective part of it, the descriptor that gets placed in front of "artist." Using a word as a verb may give it more power, more economy or authority.

AF: Language is malleable. What matters is who is saying it, and in what sense. To call something feminist, to call something queer, can mean a very different thing depending on who's saying it. And I think when it's, say, a mainstream newspaper, it tends to be reductive and negative. When we feel that these words that we have cared a lot about are being reduced, we think, *how dare you* .... Maybe that work is "feminist," but that description isn't enough. Some of this language has been used to the point that it has been nullified.

LPZ: Well, it has become marketing. It's used to boost gallery sales, in the most cynical sense.

AF: It gives the gallery a check mark, it gives the critic a check mark. Part of what I wanted to bring up is that when I wrote in "How to Review Art as a Feminist" that I was going on strike, it meant I'm leaving an industry, I'm leaving a job. I didn't want to build a career there, which I think goes back to the idea of critics speaking the truth. Take the "Hide and Seek" show [discussed in Goldberg's *The Estrangement Principle*]—it was revered in every publication, but it was a shit show. Why didn't anyone say anything? They didn't want to piss off [cocurator] Jonathan Katz.

AG: I said something, but many years later, in a book...

AF: But no one cares!

AG: Yeah, Holland Cotter didn't pan it in the *New York Times*.

AF: It was offensive. People write about people they want to associate themselves with, so that they can snowball. But they're not being honest.

AG: Going back to the first question about how I realized I couldn't control or critique if artists themselves wanted to call their work queer or were creating spaces they said were queer art spaces.... It's a lot about who's putting the label on what writer or institution. Obama was President for the entire time period during which I wrote this book. There were lots of instances where there was a shift between queerness being fully rejected by the state and being fully palatable, and there were similar issues in the United States around race. I was thinking about my position in relation to those shifts. In a lot of *The Estrangement Principle*, I was thinking, when we use the word "queer," how is that then making queerness somehow exceptional? Queer communities are still struggling with the same issues around white supremacy and being inside of all these colonial systems of power, in the United States and in art communities in particular. I felt like I was critiquing queerness, critiquing my communities, and it felt very risky. Then, over the course of writing this book, I realized that I had been acting totally paranoid. I realized it was really generous that I was trying to map this process of making a community.

WRITING THROUGH THE LENS OF DISABILITY CULTURE

EMILY WATLINGTON

As an art critic who writes primarily about disability culture and accessibility, I'm often doing mental gymnastics—especially when I'm aware that I am speaking to both disabled and nondisabled audiences. I know that the majority of art magazine readers are not versed in terms and concepts from the disability justice movement, and for now, I'm prioritizing the task of explaining them. I am proud to do this work—it's important! But it isn't always creatively fulfilling, repeating again and again that, say, disabled people do in fact enjoy our lives sometimes, and that we'd love to be able to access art. Worse, it can be depressing that I still need to say these things. I know that many of the artists I write about share this dilemma too.

To make things even more complicated, much of the terminology is also controversial within the community. For example, plenty of disabled people prefer to use person-first language, which is to say, they prefer the phrase "person with a disability" over "disabled person." But opponents feel that this treats "disabled" as a dirty word. I agree with the dissenting opinion, and there's usually not enough space to explain all that, though I can't say I am speaking neutrally when I know I'm using terminology that many disagree with. When writing a short review of an exhibition by a disabled artist, I could easily eat up all my space explaining the terms. Similarly, if I were to comment on every inaccessible component of many exhibitions, my critiques could usually fill up my word count. I often repeat that I care about access not only for its own sake, but because I also care about the art that's worth accessing.

As a person who isn't visibly disabled, I know most people assume that I am not. And though I want the disability community to know that they can, to a degree, trust me—which isn't to say that they should always agree with me—I also usually don't feel comfortable disclosing my medical information. Often, when you say you are disabled, people want to know what your diagnosis is, so they can decide whether it's really a disability or not. I think about this in decisions as seemingly simple as whether to use "they" or "we" when referring to disabled people in my writing. Though it's important to me to identify as part of this group, my identification has sometimes led to awkward conversations with editors.

Access evangelism can also be tiring. Often, instead, I try to allow accessibility to inform my writing method, even when I write about unrelated topics. One practice is known as "plain language." Some academic publications, especially in the field of disability studies, will commission a plain language translation by a trained expert—a text that's supposed to be more accessible to people with certain cognitive disabilities. The idea is simply to avoid jargon, or phrases like "the former" and "the latter" that ask the reader to return to a different point in the text and make it easy to get lost. Crucially, penning plain language does not mean dumbing down the message; it means striving for clarity and concision. I try to write in plain language from the start rather than translate something after the fact—though I'm not above making exceptions for that perfect yet obscure adjective, or a tempting alliteration. After all, in no text does every reader know every word and reference, and rich, complicated language has its place. For example, the practice of vividly describing artworks for blind and low vision people—known as image descriptions or, if online, alt text—also informs my writing. I always try to imagine that the reader has not seen the work and cannot see images of it. Both frameworks are useful for art writers everywhere.

Some disabled artists share my political agenda but offend my personal taste or artistic sensibilities. I've avoided covering them—though I'm always happy to see a disabled artist succeed, I don't want to reinforce the ableist trope of being impressed that they could make art at all, thereby holding them to lesser standards. Disabled artists are also often rewarded by nondisabled audiences when their artwork explains ordinary aspects of their lives—like, this is how I tie my shoe as a one-handed person. Some versions of this work disappoint me, because it too easily feeds into another ableist trope of being impressed and inspired when someone manages to "overcome" their impairment, but then again, many people do need those initial moments of realization that, say, some people in wheelchairs can in fact dance quite well! Given a general reader's understanding of disability at this time, I don't feel that publicly saying "this work by a disabled artist you've never heard of is politically important but formally weak" is productive for the struggle. And while the disability community is extremely supportive, I often wish that there were more disabled art critics with different taste than mine!

Disability demands that we adapt our norms, and adaptation is often creatively generative. I can't wait until we have to do a little less educating so we can unleash all these creative forces.

POINTS OF REFERENCE AND BELONGING
ANDY CAMPBELL

In my failure to compartmentalize two concurrent pieces of writing, I am thinking about the topic of this essay—comparative references to other artists as an enduring component of art criticism—alongside a recent gallery show of photographs by Mark McKnight that

> *depict, in high-contrast black-and-white, moments of beatific calm in the midst of carnal frenzy.*

I'm often in the situation of writing a review while working on a longer text, so this concurrence is not unusual. Yet now I am self-consciously deconstructing a part of my process as I enact it, and along the way intentionally articulating to myself the range of reasons for referencing the practices of other artists.

Any reference to another artist's work in the context of a review is an intentional conceptual displacement of the practice or work being reviewed; it transports a reader along a temporary guyline to an alternative point in the constellated space-time of visual practices. Depending on how such references are used, they can enrich or flatten the work being discussed. In their most generous form, such references can support the idea of discursive syncopation across practices; in their most damning, though, they can suggest the reviewed work is derivative or only apropos to certain formal, thematic, or process-based conversations.

In some of McKnight's images, two bearish brown guys fuck and play in a landscape recognizable to me as the Coachella Valley. There's a rough 'n' sweet quality to these interactions, and McKnight counterbalances their tone by interspersing photographs of cloud-laden skies or minor, dramatic features in the desert's topography.

I knew, almost as soon as I saw the work, that I wanted to mention Laura Aguilar

> *for her technical precision and for the discerning placement of her own queer, fat, and brown body in the dramatic desert landscapes of California's Coachella Valley.*

While Aguilar's photographs are dynamos of intimate encounters—familial, platonic, social, mythic, and, yes, erotic—their registers are certainly distinct from those of McKnight's work, which can veer into the pornographic. On that score, his efforts recall

> *the polymathic [Jack] Fritscher, the gonzo writer, sometime photographer, and former editor of* Drummer *(the watershed leather publication that did much to deliver BDSM into the hands, hearts, and dungeons of many a fledgling kinkster).*
>
> *Like Fritscher, McKnight serves us editorial sex.*

By mentioning Aguilar and Fritscher in this way, together and in close succession, I hope to explicitly argue that

> *both contributed to the cultural and communal sensibilities underlying the unrepentantly queer expressions that McKnight, and those similarly attuned, make prodigious use of today.*

Here I want to insist on the multiplicity and capaciousness of a queer visuality that McKnight's work could be contextualized within. Yet I am cognizant of a much wider and effulgent tradition in queer (male) photography wherein eroticized bodies—usually male—are offered as an accompaniment to, or perhaps the ultimate example of, a sense of personal liberation. To this end, I include mentions of Bob Mizer and Tom Bianchi in the review as well. Bianchi was my editor's suggestion—and one that I initially rejected, because Bianchi's photographs have largely portrayed

> *the palpable joy and sexual energy of normatively attractive gay men,*

something that McKnight's work abjures through the artist's choice of models, framing, process, materiality, and scale. There's maybe too much difference between Bianchi and McKnight, and forcing the comparison seemed to flatten (as previously mentioned) what is a more complex affective and sexual terrain in McKnight's work. But, given that I put Bianchi's mention at the end of the review, after several other practices had already been discussed, my fears seemed unjustified upon self-examination. I let the edit stay. Revision is full of such dramas (for some writers this may not be so, but for me it is); I pick where I push back on an edit selectively.

I can also identify a not-so-queer history to McKnight's visual strategies. One of the photographs in the show

> *inevitably called to mind Alfred Stieglitz's sublime photographs of clouds (the "Equivalents" series, 1922–34), which [Stieglitz] believed "put down my philosophy of life—to show that [the success of] my photographs [was] not due to subject matter—not to special trees, or faces, or interiors, to special privileges, clouds were there for everyone—no tax as yet on them—free."*

And although the novelty of the subject of queer sex—heroically centralized in McKnight's work—initially had me assuming that the artist's approach was fundamentally different from the kind of photographic modernism Stieglitz practiced, I think as I write that it is worth articulating how McKnight's work extends *and* diverges from this inherited visual canon. In other words, it is not enough to articulate an "other" tradition of queer photographic practices; it is also important to connect this with non-queer artistic practices where it seems appropriate.

But this raises a question: Am I mentioning Stieglitz to shore up, or to otherwise give gravitas to, McKnight's photographs? Considering the other artists I'm mentioning, many of whom are not at all canonical within survey histories of photography, I don't think so. Were Stieglitz to be the only point of reference, a reader might come to the conclusion that I was trying to build an equivalence between two photographers working nearly one hundred years apart. But to determine whether or not this really is the case, I return to my quoted source, the photographer's luminous and crabby essay "How I Came to Photograph Clouds" (1923)—a response, of sorts, to some of his critics who believed his success was merely attributable to the "hypnotic" powers he held over his subjects. Against such nebulous claptrap Stieglitz lands a devastating rhetorical blow at the end of his essay: "My aim is increasingly to make my photographs look so much like photographs that unless one has *eyes* and *sees*, they won't be seen—and still everyone will never forget them having once looked at them." Stieglitz ends with patronizing truculence, "I wonder if that is clear."

He's all in a snit, but it *is* clear. At least to me. This impossible position of being simultaneously unseen and unforgettable aligns with what I'm seeing as generative in McKnight's work. Yet while this condition may be consonant, McKnight's strategy differs significantly:

> *when an upturned hollow of a fallen tree is given the title* Untitled (Tree Void), *a viewer is meant to make the morphological connection between a log, a dick, and an asshole; the deadwood becomes remarkable through its purposeful concatenation with images of bodies and their orifices.*

One of the reasons that I took on this review in the first place was that I felt I knew enough to provide a useful description and assessment of the work. My own research into queer communities, with particular attention to visualizations of kinky sex, means that I have gathered an internal "call sheet" of artists who address identity, sex, and pornography on a regular basis. Sometimes these artists are making work with full cognizance of one another, at other times the lineage is more of a sensed community—a set of impulses shared by a generation or between them.

And so, nearing the end of my review, I can't help myself. I have more artists to mention—some well-known in the pages of the magazine I'm writing for, but many not. I want to address not only McKnight's work, but also its editorial framing, using my capacity as a contributor to contemporary art discourse to pressurize the kind of work deemed *worthy* of discussion.

My desire to reference has escalated. (Because I have been intentionally thinking about it? Probably.)

The word count is too constrictive.... No time to situate, only list...

> *But that these photographs function reasonably well as porn and as art suggests their placement within a broader lineage of homosexy work, because to understand some*

of the visual language and queer symbolism McKnight employs requires a concomitant knowledge not only of Aguilar's and Fritscher's output, but also of the works of Alvin Baltrop, Lanee Bird, Rick Castro, John Preston, Efren Ramirez, Rink, Jim Stewart, and Lou Thomas's Target Studios, to name only a few. McKnight belongs to this motley storied history of picturing queer sex.

ON SMALLNESS: THE POISE AND POLITICS OF CAPITAL LETTERS

ASHLEY STULL MEYERS

An often-repeated bit of lore in my family came to me by way of my father, at as early an age as I can remember. "If you've got nothing else in this world, you've got your name." It's a sentiment widely held within Black southern households like the one embodied by generations of Louisiana Stulls. It's a point of self-defined dignity within a society built on structural indignities toward nonwhite communities.

Though this piece of advice was given in reference to our surname, I hold it close, as it pertains to the way I reference other, less intimate families to which I also belong. In addition to the names handed down in my family tree, I also inherited the name Black.

My Black, rural roots have made me particularly sensitive to language that's diminutive. If you want to get a rise out of my father or uncles, grown men who have persevered through everything from the latter years of Jim Crow to 1980s-era respectability politics, call them "boy." Call them anything outside of their family-given names, with the aim of connoting smallness.

In recent years, various editorial style guides have come to recognize, either through political necessity or politeness, the value of capitalizing the titles of cultural communities, including Black, Latiné, or Indigenous. In 2020, media outlets like the *New York Times*, the *Associated Press*, the *Washington Post*, and the *Atlantic* all formally revised their standards to officially recognize "Black" (in reference to diasporic peoples of African ancestry) as distinct from the descriptor of the color—the descriptor for darkness. For me, the case against the lowercase *black* is even simpler. It's the desire for the word to hold a visual weight representative of the weight (and pride) I feel in writing from a culture of resilience—from the position of a voice only made possible by generations of others who refused to be quieted.

As in all valuable discourse, a good many Black thinkers that I deeply respect will disagree. They may state a valid and generous proposition for resisting "Blackness" as the monolith that an uppercase *B* may suggest. Some will argue that part of the project of a communal recentering and reclamation of "black" is the resistance to an oversimplified rhetoric around a culture that is rhizomatic and diasporic, or that using the lowercase *b* is a form of resistance to the great many things that colonial influence deemed "civilized" or appropriate. I'm partially persuaded. There are no simple answers or inherent truths when discussing the growth and evolution of language. As a writer and editor, I am beholden to language as a dynamic project, an unyielding investigation, a daily practice within which one needs the humility to admit incompleteness and the gumption to continue to reach for something a little better. The quest can feel both romantic and maddening. But what continues to arise as a surefire best practice is to err on the side of honor. While Black teachers and makers will forever be entitled to subvert and revise a canon of language founded in the colonialist suppression of otherness, the publications and structures that thrive within that canon owe a debt of revision.

Contemporary editorial practice should be steeped in care, elasticity, an artful consideration of what words can signify, and a willingness to move forward from "norms" that no longer suit. It should be critical, but critical in favor of the best in human impulse.

"If you've got nothing else, you've got your name."

In the absence of the most common decencies, people from marginalized positions hold tight to the words that reference their communities and lineages—the loving and sometimes secret names by which generations of our ancestors were internally referenced. In opposition to the painfully creative onslaught of diminutive terms crafted by those who would make us small, we have something else. The African diaspora has Black.

EDITING AND PUBLISHING

How can editors advocate for a more equitable field and better working conditions?

What are some common issues editors address with writers, and what does healthy communication look like?

What alternative forms and functions of publishing can we imagine?

How do writers decide which publications to contribute to, and how does that affect what they write about?

HOW TO FOSTER A HEALTHY WRITER-EDITOR RELATIONSHIP

ELISA WOUK ALMINO

As someone who is both a writer and an editor, I understand what it's like to be on both sides of the writer-editor relationship. Like all relationships, it can be about chemistry: some people might click really well, others not so much. But each party can do some basic things to maintain a healthy relationship—one that feels both respectful and productive. I'll focus here on what editors can do. While this list is not exhaustive, it should serve as a starting point for building a relationship that centers care.

1. Fine-tune the pitch. Ideally—especially in a new writer-editor relationship—you wouldn't just green-light a pitch without giving some feedback and direction. Have a conversation with the writer before they set out to write. Collaborating at this first stage can be really crucial; it's your opportunity to help shape the piece and set expectations (like word count, which should always be on the lower end, as writers love to go over—I'm guilty as charged).
2. Be deliberate when you commission stories. Consider writers who understand the work's or artist's context or who have a history of engaging with the topic or subject. (That said, it's worth sometimes pushing writers outside their comfort zones and usual interests; avoid having the same voices weigh in on the same topics.) Be curious toward the writers you're working with—ask them what they've been thinking about, what kinds of assignments they might be interested in. Assign local writers to cover local topics when possible,

and if that's not an option, make sure they're in conversation with people who might be. The bottom line here: be mindful of the voices and perspectives you are bringing into your publication.

3. This might sound basic, but once a piece is sent your way, make your edits in tracked changes—don't just hack away at it without leaving any trace. Try to make your edits more of a conversation. For example, in addition to making line edits, I also leave plenty of comments. I ask pointed questions and clarify intent—I try to suggest alternatives rather than just make the changes outright.
4. Think about how *you* would want someone to convey feedback. Don't just point out what needs work. Comment on the things that move you, surprise you, etc.
5. Don't be afraid of asking questions and coming across as "stupid." If something is unclear to you, chances are that it will be to a lot of other readers.
6. Be aware of your shortcomings and know your strengths. This might mean holding your ground when it comes to grammar but acknowledging when you might be misreading something or don't have the context that the author does (they often have an area of expertise you don't). This could be a case where you ask questions rather than immediately make cuts or changes.
7. Be communicative. Acknowledge receipt when a writer files their piece. Let them know if you are swamped or when they can expect edits so that they're not left worrying sick about being ghosted. Try not to let a piece sit in your inbox for weeks (I generally aim to take a first pass the same week the piece is filed, if possible).
8. Especially if you're working with freelancers, be considerate of their time and the fact that they are

probably juggling a million assignments that you don't know about.

9. Be an advocate for the writers you work with. When writers are doing good work, share that with other editors and your supervisors. Make a case for higher pay rates when you can. Higher rates make it possible for a more diverse set of people to contribute to your publication.

Finally, as editors, we want to help writers grow; we want to challenge them and get their work into the best shape possible. My last two points of advice apply to editing art criticism in particular:

10. Hold writers accountable to being clear and honest. This means flagging jargon and asking writers to be direct about their opinions. In other words, don't let them sound like a press release—remind them that they have a voice.
11. Which leads me to my final point: encourage writers to be critical. Rather, let them know *it's okay to be* critical. I can't count the number of writers who have hesitated to criticize a project or exhibition because they think they'll be banned from the art world. My response is usually along the lines of: Write a critical piece when you have something to say—because your argument has stakes and feels important. But don't avoid criticism out of fear of hurting someone's feelings.

When writer-editor relationships are broken, it's often because of the pressures of publishing in today's frenzied media landscape. It's not easy to be an editor, but try not to let the stress get in the way. It's vital for editors to be in solidarity with writers because we are a conduit to getting them published, heard, and paid. As editors, we also have power in terms of which narratives get published—it's a big responsibility, so it's important to be intentional. The quality of what we put out in the world will only be better if we have healthy, honest, and communicative relationships with the writers we work with.

WORON (AN ARTIST'S APPROACH TO WRITING AND EDITING): A MANIFESTO

KRISTINA KAY ROBINSON

I write in a long tradition of writers like me. I descend from an infinite line of composers, conductors, inventors.

The cosmology of the Bambara—a Mandé people native to Mali who made up a larger portion of the enslaved population in Louisiana than in any other part of the Western Hemisphere—is described in some detail in Gwendolyn Midlo Hall's *Africans in Colonial Louisiana*: "According to this cosmology, the universe, emerging from a moving void, undergoes a slow process of acquiring voice and vibration that eventually evolves into light, sound, creatures, actions, and human sentiments." After the collapse of the Malian empire, the Bambara emigrated into the Senegambia region. Their philosophical disposition was therefore cultivated by movement; it lent itself to cultural retention even amid the horrors of the transatlantic slave trade. In *Flash of the Spirit*, Robert Farris Thompson examines the Mandekan word *woron*. Literally meaning "to get the kernel," it encapsulates the process needed to master speech, song, music, or any aesthetic endeavor. Applying this term to writing art criticism, I try to understand in the simplest terms what I want to communicate about my subject. I start with three sentences that, even if they don't make it to the final draft, help me build its layers. The goal is to be creative with syntax and still craft readable prose that provokes an emotional response in the reader and gives them something new to consider. It's an approach to mastery not as the pursuit of perfection but as an intellectual transformation for the editor, writer, and reader. Thompson goes on to outline the Mandé concept of reason, which relies on a balance between *badenya* (the conformist) and *fadenya* (the innovator). This tension between tradition and innovation produces a culture always in flux, always moving, changing, and reinventing the world.

Yet—

I write as an impossibility.

Black women born and educated in the Deep South are a recent arrival, and still a rarity in the discipline of art criticism. I was born on the Gulf Coast, in New Orleans. I have chosen, thus far, to try to participate in this industry while living here. According to the United States' most potent mythologies created during Hurricane Katrina, I am the left behind—a metaphor, a historical occurrence, a phenomenon, or an object; I am a vessel to be studied, eulogized, bemoaned, deified, and vilified by the artist, writer, or critic who will deliver their perspective. It is possible to learn from but not be instructed by a person like me.

How then does someone from such a position of culturally imposed impossibility make their way as a writer? How does this experience not limit but enhance my ability to both create and critique the work of my times? How do Black women, femmes, and gender non-conforming people insert their grammars, perspectives, counter-logics, cultures, and conclusions into public discourse? How did it happen for me? How can I use my own path-in-progress to examine the structure, forecast the future, and move in ways that are beneficial individually and collectively? For me, beyond formal education, this process began from a radical self-declaration: my perspective matters, my thoughts are important, and I don't need anyone to give me permission to exist in the landscape of arts and letters. This approach is grounded in the Mandekan principles of *badenya* and *fadenya*. Alongside pursuing traditional means of publication, one of my most critical professional decisions was to publish and curate independently. This allowed me to build a body of work grounded in my own scholarship and to cultivate a perspective that has served me in institutional settings as well.

I have developed what I call an ethics of the avant-garde in my approach to critique, form, and vocabulary as both a writer and editor. This is not the notion of the avant-garde as defined by Western canonical art history but rather as informed by principles like *badenya* and *fadenya*. I can approach my work with a dedication to maintaining certain structures, principles, and ethics as provided by *badenya*, while embracing the dynamism suggested by *fadenya*. I think of *badenya* in criticism as the nuts and bolts: clarity of prose, consistency of grammar and punctuation, and support of theses and ideas that are revisited and clarified in the conclusion of a piece. *Badenya* also manifests as a consistent and ethical citational practice, while *fadenya* calls for expanding the archive to properly credit and compensate the work of those often marginalized by the canon.

The following are a few of my working rules and reminders to carry *badenya* and *fadenya* into my writing and editing practice:

Make no assumptions or presumptions about the content. I begin by making note of a work's features and what responses, emotional or intellectual, it evokes for me as I experience it. I then move on from these thoughts to consider the curatorial statement, artist's statement, other reviews, etc., and how these ideas converge with and diverge from one another.

Resist crafting a hierarchy of perspectives. White supremacy has produced a canon of art history that is exclusionary and incomplete. To counter this version of events, we will require new ways of thinking about sight and an expanded vocabulary to render a more just and equitable archive.

Accept and expect thoughtful edits.

Ask more questions; make less prescriptive word choice edits.

Embrace the unique syntaxes of human speech. Allow English as a language to grow; let it do new things on the page. I embrace the conventions of my speech patterns that emerge out of Southern Louisiana. I tend to favor compound sentences and repetition. I like to bring in words from other languages (such as French, Arabic, Kouri-Vini, Haitian Kreyol, and the Mandé language family) that have influenced the worldviews of my immediate environment. I think translation is important. I also think that the comingling of languages and the artistic principles of non-Western canons can play a role in creating new approaches to writing about contemporary art. These new approaches might be centered on accepting the opacity that this comingling of languages can introduce, while fostering the emergence of new ideas, theories, and ways of seeing. Allowing space for difference can also support, rather than hinder, mutual intelligibility and the development of new and exciting visual languages.

Pay more attention to shape's ability to guide and enhance meaning. I think of the essay as a poetic form. The shape of the poem, whether formal or free verse, can be as important a decision for the poet to make as specific word choices. So, how an essay is structured is important to my creative process. It is also a part of the principle of *fadenya* that allows me more freedom in my content without losing the reader.

Consider that you might be wrong.

Thwart expectations. Leaving the reader with something new to consider is essential to my application of *woron*, of getting to the kernel. We have increasing opportunities to create and disseminate writing that is resistant to the conventions, constraints, and limitations of racial, economic, and state borders and allegiances. I work for the disruption of current formulas and a return to the imagination—the force that Amiri Baraka, in "The Revolutionary Theatre," called a "practical vector from the soul." From that mysterious void in each of us can emerge a voice that will inspire action and light.

WORD CHOICE: WHO'S YOUR AUDIENCE HERE?
DESSANE LOPEZ CASSELL

A false binary is often proposed in art writing: complex ideas aren't (or can't be) accessible. Beyond being unimaginative, this framework lays bare assumptions that have shaped the field for decades. It posits that vocabulary and experiences not rooted in the academy—or other exclusive realms—are somehow lacking; that skillful, expressive writing about art and culture requires SAT words and references to critical theory. Neither could be more untrue. Still, the myth persists.

As a writer who is also an editor, I have a few ideas about what lies behind this stubborn hold. The practical difficulties of navigating the field feel particularly pertinent: chalk it up to the impostor syndrome that flares after every unsuccessful pitch or grant application; or the sting of watching those less talented (yet better connected) succeed while you sit in purgatory. When your "voice" can't seem to catch a break (or help you pay rent), it can be tempting to rely on the same old styles of jargon that seem to have helped others do well. Less cynically speaking, the over reliance on the esoteric can also stem from a desire to connect myriad dots—to build bridges where others haven't yet—albeit not always legibly.

Playing the editor's card again, let's consider another method. What if we approached art criticism from the position of inviting (more) readers in, instead of (even unintentionally) appealing to those already initiated? Much as my colleague Laura Raicovich has advocated in art museums, my agenda—as a writer, editor, and reader—is to make art writing engaging for more people.[1] This aim goes hand in hand with ongoing calls to decolonize art institutions and loosen the grip of toxic philanthropy. If readers can't engage with what we're writing, can we really expect them to feel invested in it?

To be clear, this is not a call to eliminate nuance, or uniqueness of voice or vision. Rather, it's a vote in favor of scaffolding—an approach that breaks new concepts and information into digestible chunks, strategically building upon each one.[2] This method, first proposed by the psychologist Lev Vygotsky and later popularized in the West by educators, can help writers build those aforementioned bridges, enabling points of connection between complex ideas.

Much as effective, memorable teaching requires great skill, so too does writing of the same caliber. At the end of the day, do you *really* need to pepper your writing with terms like "gesamtkunstwerk" and "dialectic"? Does every point of contrast need to be labeled a "juxtaposition" or "dichotomy"? There's more skill in distilling intricate ideas into precise yet legible forms, particularly ones that can be understood in a variety of registers.

> [Editor's comment]
> *You're relying a little heavily on description here. I'd like to see you bring in a bit more analysis. What are the implications of [subject at hand]?*

Above is a note I often give to writers. The question of how much faith a writer is willing to invest in their audience is intertwined with these issues of accessible language. Giving readers the tools to understand an argument—which all writing is, at its core—doesn't require spoon-feeding or pulling one's punches.

While it's common to take a linear approach to crafting analysis—bringing in reams of description before leaving the reader with a zinger—some of the most compelling writing styles weave description and analysis together. Focusing on an artwork's most salient details (and then building outward from there), for example, offers one mode of blending these two features together, enabling descriptive elements to work in service of analytical ones. Each adjective choice reveals another layer of the argument at hand. The cumulative effect immediately invites me into the writer's frame of reference, better positioning me to make sense of their argument, whether or not I agree with it.

> [Editor's comment]
> *It feels worth adding more context for this point. How does this relate to broader patterns/discussions of the work?*

As writers, we can't be astute or even "objective"—for those who still believe in that fraught journalistic adage—without giving readers the tools to understand the facts at hand. Context, as the saying goes, is everything. Sure, an artist might make frequent use of certain formal strategies, but it's worth asking whether a reader's understanding of the work would be the same if they knew, for example, how the strategy in question relates to a broader historical or social context. Would a reader be able to glean the full significance of the work without more information about not only *how* it was made, but under what conditions it was meant to be presented? Context, in this sense, offers another means of instilling and illuminating nuance.

At its core, the critical work we do as writers lies in giving readers the tools to perceive what we perceive, to understand both the artist's intent and our frames of reference. A better, more equitable world—at least as far as art and culture is concerned—becomes possible the more these tools are made readily available.

1 Laura Raicovich, *Culture Strike: Art and Museums in an Age of Protest* (New York: Verso, 2021).

2 Dawn Castagno-Dysart, Bryan Matera, and Joel Traver, "The Importance of Instructional Scaffolding," *Teacher Magazine,* April 23, 2019, https://www.teachermagazine.com/au_en/articles/the-importance-of-instructional-scaffolding.

MIRA DAYAL: We've been talking about studio critiques and how, with "soft talk," you're denying the presence of any single authority figure, in the sense that you're allowing people to bring their own subjective associations to the work without assuming that there's any single viewpoint that is the proper reading or any proper background that is required to access the work. This also relates to the question of solidarity in the sense that you're not necessarily equipped with all the proper tools to access every work that everyone is making, but allowing different people to access the work from different contexts or situations or preconceptions is important and necessary, and doesn't happen enough.

ANNIE GODFREY LARMON: There are many differences between the kinds of criticism we're talking about—studio critiques versus art reviews—but with reviews, there's literally an author. Someone is offering a position. So, maybe a question here is how to develop an authorial voice that is also deferential to, or generative of, or incorporates, as many readings as possible, while also providing a voice that the reader knows to trust for a responsible or reliable framework through which to think about something. So, rather than, you know, returning to Barbara

Rose and Rosalind Krauss, or the idea that there is a measurable standard against which all objects should be judged, how do we think of a responsible voice that we trust to navigate difference to understand various conditions, whether on the basis of what they're bringing to the table in terms of education or experience, or identity? How do we negotiate that author function while ceding the idea of authority at the same time?

LESLIE DICK: Part of the problem is how to make space for multiple perspectives and multiple experiences while creating the sustained, repeated, trustworthy voice. Of course, there are people we always want to read because we enjoy what they say, or how they say it, or what books and ideas they bring to bear on whatever they are writing about. But one of the biggest problems we have right now is that we're all reading the people we trust. How do you get a complicated discourse that has multiple perspectives based on different experiences? I'm very aware that everything I do is predicated on the fact that I have a full-time teaching job. This privilege allows me time to write about the things that really interest me. Because I have a paycheck—it comes in once a month!

AUDIENCE: And at very credible institutions.

You've spoken about CalArts and Yale, and both yield so much power. I'd be curious if you could speak about that.

MD: And a sense of responsibility and accountability that comes with that power.

AGL: I think that's where this intimate space of discourse has an opportunity to have a much broader reach. That's also what I've been trying to speak to—the power that the critic wields is to grant access to a work that maybe doesn't have the support structures of an institution or an Ivy League pedigree, or best friends at certain galleries or art advisories. What writing can do is open something up—it's an amplifier, and in that sense, it wields power.

LD: Absolutely. Writing is an amplifier. And I want there to be more voices and more positions to speak from. To me, solidarity is always about standing in a kind of collectivity, acknowledging difference, which may take the form of conflict or even fundamental disagreement. I mean, the person living in the mansion standing in solidarity with the striking dock workers is not saying, "I am a striking dock worker," right? They're not saying, "I'm the same as you," or even, "I understand you." They're saying that their limited experience in terms of class position is radically different from yours, but intellectually they completely support your project, and they're going to write a check, or they're going to march in the street, or call their friend who's a politician—that's what solidarity looks like. It's about standing together across difference, and I'm very invested in the idea that being present together and acknowledging that kind of difference is the only way that we're going to change the world.

AUDIENCE: I think that's a very important thing to say, because if there's a rigid identity politics that doesn't allow for that kind of broad solidarity with difference, if one is only allowed to write from whatever class position, religion, race, nationality, then what doesn't happen? Any one doesn't read the other.

LD: Yes. I see it this way: I can never understand your experience fully. It's going to be an incomplete understanding. But we have this thing called language, and language is so precious because it tries to do something with that incompleteness.

We can talk to each other, across difference, and maybe build a partial, incomplete understanding together. The time and space to do this kind of work are themselves a privilege, and I'm aware that studying at august institutions like CalArts and Yale is a very expensive way to materialize that time and space. Fortunately, there are a lot of other ways to do it, and we have to show up for that work, in all sorts of contexts and situations.

AGL: And, of course, under different conditions and across time, solidarity has meant very different things. When there are fewer artists who are women who are showing, there are fewer women critics writing, and maybe that situation calls for celebration in a way. But now we have a surplus of women artists, and MFA pipelines are full of them—whether they're getting attention or reviews or showing or being paid is a different question.

NEWS FOR HOME: NAVIGATING ART CRITICISM FOR GENERAL AUDIENCES

JILLIAN STEINHAUER

When I quit my job in the fall of 2017, I went looking for proof of concept. I'd spent several years as an editor at a widely read art publication, but what I wanted was to go mainstream. Was it partly so that more people would read my work? Undoubtedly. But it was about more than ego. I was driven by this strange, surprisingly persistent conviction that contemporary art could and should matter to more people than just art insiders—that art has a lot to say to those who aren't necessarily listening.

Surveying the media landscape before I went freelance, I saw major newspapers and magazines that regularly covered movies but only ran the occasional, often uninformed piece about art. I looked frustratedly at publications that had eliminated the positions of their art critics, if they'd ever had them at all, and others that had kept those jobs but only for those who have long held such positions—often white people over the age of sixty. I wondered what it might look like for a young, socially and politically engaged—albeit still white—writer like myself to try to bring art into these spaces that seemed disinterested. Could I get them and their readers to trust me and to care?

Superficially, the answer has been yes. Over the past few years, I've written reviews, essays, profiles, and features about art and artists for several national general-interest publications, some regularly. As I suspected, it is possible. Whether or not it's been successful is harder to say. Have

I convinced anyone to learn more, to visit museums or galleries? Do my stories generate significant responses or sizable traffic? I mostly don't know.

What I do know is that writing about art—which is highly specialized, with multiple languages of its own—for a general audience is harder than I'd expected. You can't assume that the reader has any context for the work, and you can't draw from a well of shared experiences; you have to spell out some of the field's most fundamental ideas. This means I spend a lot of my space describing and explaining, which leaves less room for thinking and analysis. I worry that my criticism isn't rigorous enough by art-world standards or that it's too obscure for a general reader—or that it may be both. A piece that's too basic for a curator might still be hard to follow for my cousin who's an accountant and subscribes to the *New York Times*, and yet I know both might be reading. My coping method is to focus on ideas—both my own and the ones in the work—rather than hypothesizing my audience and trying to split the difference.

Ideas, too, are one of the ways I've been able to pique the interest of editors who don't assign a lot of art pieces. These editors aren't especially interested in debates about the death of painting or materiality, but they can recognize conceptual savvy or a good story. I tend to pitch writing about artists whose work or lives have something to say about the wider world, so that the lessons I draw are more broadly applicable. I envision these pieces as part of a larger conversation and set of questions—asked by me and countless others—about how we understand our own history and society.

I have no real desire to write for art publications these days. I understand their value and sometimes envy the complexity they afford their writers, but for me, talking to a mainstream audience is the greater, more appealing challenge. Writing about art feels, more than ever, like an act of translation. I'm simultaneously serving as an interpreter, a guide, and an evaluator. The process has forced me to return to the essentials, to ask myself time and again why I care about art at all, and to reevaluate what keeps me under its spell.

The answer I tend to come back to is: art can be radical. Not all of it, of course, and not always, but the conditions that make it hard to explain to a layperson are the same ones that make it a space of freedom: there aren't actually that many rules. I daresay (and I can already hear the pushback here) the baseline of contemporary art is weirder, more political, and more open-ended than that of popular forms like literature or television. Art doesn't offer an escape so much as it offers a set of possibilities for evading or reimagining or shifting the norm—something I was quietly drawn to for years but that has felt increasingly vital the older and more politically aware I become (and the messier human reality seems to be). I may not always be up to the challenge, but art gives me permission to think in a different way.

I want to extend that permission to my readers, whether they're seeking it or not. I'm never sure if I'm getting it right—if I'm telling stories both clearly and deeply enough for them to be approachable as well as thought-provoking. But when I write, especially for people who don't read much about art, what I'm saying is: Come look. This thing is worth your time. It's bizarre and beautiful in its own way and maybe a bit of bullshit too. And if you stick around long enough, if you're open, it just might change you.

LETTER FROM AN ARTS WORKER
JESSICA LYNNE

Dear DéLana,

I have been reading Lorraine Hansberry's *To Be Young, Gifted, and Black* (1969), her informal autobiography that is peppered with her letters to the people for whom she cared the most. The people who knew her, who saw her wince and draft and revise. The people who knew how deeply she loved writing and Chicago and Black folks.

Selfishly, I have been thinking about our own ongoing exchanges of epistles. How we have been watching one another wince and draft and revise. How we are now at another place of revision. How we are approaching another threshold trying to find the language for this transgression. And it certainly seems to me that transgression is the best word to use at the moment. We are crossing lines aren't we?

Are we weary? I fear this letter is going to become a series of too many questions because as I ask you these things I am really asking myself the things I am too afraid to admit. Maybe I felt an inkling of this last summer in the midst of my transition out of that Museum that couldn't quite get it together. Though I don't think I was ready to admit fatigue. But it was there, living in my body.

How do we talk about this? The mirage of sanctuary. (Is that the language we've been looking for?) Here we are: two Black women who have made our way to a new place, found family in one another, and felt a righteous calling to care for the cultural production of Black folks. I still feel that pull. It too lives in my body. But I am also thinking about the real moments of confusion or loneliness, an all too familiar story. I am honest enough to admit that I have always thought of the arts as a place of refuge. When I landed in that very Black Brooklyn arts institution after a disappointing experience in Chicago, it was a balm. Someone much wiser than I had taken a chance on my passion, and in turn, I found myself surrounded by an entire canon of art that was alive! Alive!

Here I am writing you, some years after that initial landing. Still very young, still very unsure of many things, still thinking the arts a refuge, but cautious. Some of this trepidation is what naturally happens as one ages, certainly, and yet, how else to feel, for example, after watching the recent Whitney Biennial debauchery? So many scrambling to protect the fragility of white femininity even as Black women are asking that we look closely and critically. How does one imagine a future in spaces that are only interested in you when it is convenient? Yes, I suspect we are weary of being tokenized or taken for granted or being ignored.

I have noticed how quickly people like us—young, Black arts workers—are referred to as angry, enraged, misguided. *Why don't you give us a chance*, they say. *We were hoping to spark a dialogue*, they say. *We would really love for you to sit on this panel and explain your anger to us*, they say.

I don't know girl. I'm probably rambling. The world is very frightful right now. Children are dying. Communities are being forced to drink poisoned water. People are losing the sacredness of their holy places. Police are killing us. Bombs are being dropped.

But I am trying to make sense of where I am standing. I do not want to fold underneath my silence. As *ARTS.BLACK* enters into another year of production, I am acutely aware of the potency of its imprint. That I can be clear and explicit about my frustrations *and also* vulnerable here is a fact for which I am always grateful. It offers its own kind of freedom much like BAI offered its own kind of freedom. It was for everyone but it was also *ours*. These are the instances that pull me forward.

So when you ask me where we go next, I will tell you that we should go where we are loved. We go where there is a respect for our entire being, for the histories and spirits that enter with us as we enter into a place. We go where there is an insistence on recognizing that art helps us map our pasts, presents, and futures. We go to a place that will remind us to breathe, to drink water, to take care of ourselves. We go where we are *seen.* We go where we are valued. All this to say that in spite of my doubts, I am holding onto this truth:

It is possible to fashion the places that will hold us. It is possible to build the pyramids.

In solidarity,
Jess

This article first appeared as Jessica Lynne, "Letter from an Arts Worker," *ARTS.BLACK,* April 18, 2017, https://arts.black/essays/2017/04/a-letter-from-an-arts-worker-jessica-lynne/.

MIRA DAYAL: Jessica, in "Letter From an Arts Worker," which was published in 2017 in the publication you founded, *ARTS.BLACK*, you write about a "mirage of sanctuary" in the arts where they appear to be a place of refuge; you also write about being frustrated by the art spaces you've worked in, which do not always support you. You mention feeling a calling to care for "the cultural production of Black folks." I read this as a sort of renewal of vows for *ARTS.BLACK*. In your other writings, you have noted the importance of mentorship, emerging from a frustration with not seeing enough young Black art critics. In consideration of all these concerns, could you talk a bit more about the structure of the journal and the editorial process you've set up to make mentorship possible?

JESSICA LYNNE: *ARTS.BLACK* was founded in 2014 by me and my collaborator, Taylor Renee Aldridge. We started out as a small Tumblr, for practical reasons. We had been in conversation for months prior, thinking about what we would say as young Black women in the arts, understanding that there were other people who shared similar questions and concerns and were problem-solving in real time. *ARTS.BLACK* became an editorial container for the work that we recognized was happening but not necessarily being translated in a more "mainstream" way. We started out with two essays by friends from London and moved slowly, publishing maybe one or two pieces per month—not at the pace that the art market often demands of the criticism machine. We experimented with different structures and eventually landed on the quarterly format, twice every quarter. This allows writers to go in-depth—they don't feel that they have to turn something around in a week—but it also allows us to pay them more. As editors, we really believe in the relationship between a writer and editor, and in being embedded in the work.

MD: Merray, could you talk about *CRIT*, the publication you started, which was also intended to function outside of mainstream publications?

MERRAY GERGES: Sure—beginning with a similar set of concerns, I started a publication called *CRIT* with a couple of friends in undergrad at the Nova Scotia College of Art and Design, at a moment when the art school that I went to was in crisis. We felt that there was nowhere to talk about our frustrations as a student body and express our stresses under the administration. This was in 2012, and I think it's important to identify how the discursive moments in which we each started these publications are so different from the context in which we're operating right now. When I started *CRIT*, the conversations around consent and rape culture, for example, which are deeply embedded in how we talk about feminism and feminist solidarity now, weren't present. The student union had just started "Consent Week" and the terms of engagement were quite rudimentary. They were similarly rudimentary when it came to talking about race. Even the term "identity politics," as much as it has a deeply rooted history, wasn't a term that we knew at the time. In the art history classes that I was taking, I wasn't learning about the practices of any artists of color, so I had to teach myself. So this publication was very much concerned with trying to figure out the vocabulary. We had no idea how to talk about radical politics or systemic exclusion. The publication was a space where I could teach myself.

The political moment when all of this came about taught me a lot about relationships of care. If you don't harbor a relationship of care and trust with a writer, what are you really doing? I only learned this later, from being edited by people who edited me by saying, "Why aren't you writing this thing in this way?" That's not what an editor is supposed to do.

JL: I recognize a tendency in the more institutionally resourced art worlds to imagine that they have transcended the need for those relationships somehow. The writers I read, the writers who inform the work I'm trying to do, are committed to the politics of care in a way that goes beyond the "self care" that has been commodified. It's very easy for institutions to enact superficial gestures of "love." I knew early on that I didn't want to be in those institutions. *ARTS.BLACK* is run by two people coming from two places but with a shared responsibility and obligation that predates whatever art world we may find ourselves in and is rooted in a history of the Black radical ethos. I wanted to make sure that my writings would quote that politic, and that this publication would too. Some of those gestures included a particular type of slowness that acknowledged friendships and relationships and accountability and all of the things that make a system work well, but that were not part of the systems that I was encountering. I wasn't seeing what I wanted to see, and I recognized that I had the tools to create what I wanted to see.

MG: I started *CRIT* when I was halfway through undergrad, and I hadn't worked in the art world yet. I've since worked professionally in publishing for a number of years, and I've realized that I was already reacting against something that I didn't even understand to be the structure to react against. Now that I've worked for *Canadian Art*, which is Canada's largest contemporary art publication, I'm realizing that these ethics of care are the number one thing to go out the window within a structure that is concerned about circulation and sales. It doesn't pretend to be radical. But we don't talk enough about writer-editor relationships and how claims to solidarity fall short within that context.

MD: After you started those publications and were in the throes of working with writers as editors, how did that influence how you saw your other editing relationships? Did it affect the agency you felt you had as a writer to shape what you wrote about and how you worked with editors?

JL: I've been fortunate enough to have worked with many good editors who were diligent and patient with me but also served as mentors. And I've been in conversation with a lot of artists who are also writers, and those friendships have informed how I think about a writer's relationships. I've happily rejected the inherited or supposed belief that critics should maintain distance between themselves and artists. I recognize my mindset to be part of a particular lineage—Black folks specifically have been institutionalized *together*. That's really important. For me, the task of being an editor is connected to the task of looking closely, in the sense of not being afraid of intimacy, not being afraid to be *in it* with an artist. Looking closely is a central task I've enjoyed that has also made me a sharper writer and editor. When I work with writers on the site, I'm not afraid to be embedded in the task with them. That's something that I love about investigative journalism: You have to be in a story in a way that consumes you. I like thinking about criticism in relationality. I don't always see it treated that way. I certainly didn't see that even five years ago, when we started *ARTS.BLACK* as a place for Black writers to mature and matriculate in the system. If the art world can't hold that, I would rather be direct and deliberate about fortifying other containers.

MG: You can do that because you're willing to acknowledge power relationships and disparities within them in a way that the art world is rarely willing to do. An editor has an incredible amount of power over the writers they work with. When I started working at *Canadian Art*, I immediately developed a very antagonistic relationship with the editors I worked with because they didn't understand my work. They didn't know how to edit it, so they just sterilized the fuck out of me. I was the first person of color on editorial staff who wasn't an intern, so I was getting edited by all white editors, and I would get an entire passage cut from a text by someone who clearly didn't think about why that text was there. When I later became assistant editor, I was keen on not replicating those tensions, because I had a little bit of power. You can teach somebody how to be a good copy editor or technical editor, but you can't teach somebody so many of the other skills that are necessary to be a good editor; the key is empathy, being able to read a text and think about why a writer wrote it that way, not just about how they themselves would have written it.

JL: The two questions that I think of as I'm working with a piece, which I think are very simple questions, are, What is working? and What is not working? But behind those questions are spheres of knowledge that inform my answers. Often, we forget what types of knowledge are necessary for that writer to feel held—and not in some superficial way, but also technically. We forget that writing is a craft too. There's often an incongruence between the spheres of knowledge of the person asking those questions and the person penning the text. I recognize that everyone can't know everything, but if my role as an editor is also to be a caretaker, I need to challenge the types of knowledge that I hold. I wonder if some of our shared frustrations result from finding ourselves acquiring new knowledges—cultural and embodied—that other editors or writers are not.

FOR THE COMMA PUSHERS
DANA KOPEL

Somebody once told me that editors are typically the radical ones among museum staff. It must have been Maida Rosenstein who said it. As the president of UAW Local 2110, Maida shepherded me and my colleagues through a contentious union drive at the New Museum in 2019. She's done that for thirty years, at MoMA and elsewhere. The way librarians are often more radical, she explained—or insinuated, I can't remember—so too are editors.

I have no idea if this generalization is true. But I know that the first time I sat down with a few colleagues from the New Museum, three years ago now, to talk about how we were being exploited at work and what, concretely, we could do to change our conditions, two of the five of us were editors. Thea Ballard, my coeditor at the time and now a dear friend, knew from the start that unionizing was the only way for us workers to gain any real power at the museum. It took some others months to realize that an open letter, for instance, would offer neither the sustainability of a union nor the protections of labor law. Thea left the museum before the union campaign really got off the ground, but her replacement, Lily Bartle, became another die-hard organizer and lifelong friend.

I'm wary of the assumption that one's political efforts should be funneled through one's career. But of course, editing, like everything else, is political. For instance: At the New Museum, I created style guidelines for gendered language, and then encountered some resistance (or at least confusion) from authors when I tried to enforce them in wall texts and labels for exhibitions like Sarah Lucas's, which featured a number of sculptures of penises—and not, as curators and catalogue contributors might have it, "male genitalia," a phrase that is transphobic in its assumption that there is one correct type of "male" body. Experiences like these prompted me to think more deeply about the politics of editing. Before I was laid off, I had been speaking to my former professor, the art historian Jeannine Tang, about collaborating on a style guide addendum for art institutions to address gender and sexuality.

In general, editing is self-effacing work; a good editor disappears into the success of the text. You figure out what someone is trying to say and help them to say it more clearly, more elegantly. At the New Museum, our work was not just self-effacing but effaced by the institution as well. Even when we tried to offer thoughtful suggestions to improve the argument or legibility of a text, we were usually expected to simply copyedit or proofread, and as quickly as possible. Our work was deeply unglamorous and underappreciated: We used to say our bosses thought of us as comma pushers, moving around punctuation to make a text technically correct.

But an edited text, like a union, is a meaningful collaborative effort—a melding of individual voices into something more powerful and effective. I don't think it's the case that editors are especially suited to organizing—though I'm proud of my work on our union's communications, most of which I helped write and/or edit while I was a member—but perhaps that the nature of our work within the museum makes us particularly sensitive to the ways in which workers of all kinds are undervalued and exploited. The knowledge that nobody really cared about or even understood our work probably helped radicalize us. Certainly, I learned most of what I know about both editing and organizing from my editor-comrades at the New Museum, Thea and Lily, who taught me that our work is important, that we take care of each other, and that together, we can win. The abolitionist organizer Mariame Kaba wrote that her father used to tell her, "Everything worthwhile is done with other people." In my experience, the work of editing and the work of labor organizing both prove this sentiment true.

READING AND REFLECTING

How do writers shift their focus over time?

What prior models of publishing could guide writers in finding their own voice?

How can reflecting on past writing help writers work toward practices of repair?

What could an ethics of reading entail?

ART CRITICISM IN THE REPARATIVE MODE

ARUNA D'SOUZA

I quit writing about art sometime in 2012, at the same time as I decided to leave academia. It felt important to turn toward the world in the wake of the death of Trayvon Martin. Part of this process involved facing the realities of anti-Black violence in the United States—a history that, as a Canadian, I knew superficially, though despite having lived here for many years, had not really *understood* yet. Combine that with my status as a person of South Asian origin who misunderstood how the racism I experienced—and my capacity to succeed despite such racism—was qualitatively different from the pervasive anti-Blackness that structures US society. The racism I experienced may have knocked me down a few times in my career, but I had privilege I could not yet see. I had to learn, unlearn, and relearn at once.

The murder of Trayvon Martin ushered in what is going on nine years of heightened activism in response to state-sponsored or state-authorized executions of unarmed Black people. As I began reading more and more about the way in which white supremacy has been institutionalized in the US—including Ta-Nehisi Coates's "The Case for Reparations" (2014), a devastating accounting of the ways in which the consequences of slavery didn't end with Emancipation, but rather continued over generations to strip wealth (and therefore the capacity to access the very basic rights and institutions that we all take for granted) from Black families—I began to feel my failures as a professor acutely. While I had taught nineteenth-century European and "global" contemporary art by foregrounding questions of race, class, and gender, I still reinforced, in big and little ways, the claims that whiteness makes on culture—at best, I expanded the canon, but I did nothing to genuinely undermine or dismantle it. Worse yet, looking back, I see how unaware I was of the ways in which anti-Blackness structured and determined the lives of my students every single day, some more acutely than others. At my best moments, perhaps, I did nothing to make the situation of anti-Blackness in the classroom worse. But I could point to very few ways in which I had actively worked to undo it.

So I decided to leave academia, and become not an art critic, but a writer—a writer of what, I did not know as yet. I enjoyed writing on Facebook—which is, or at least was, a kind of micro-blogging for me. I enjoyed learning different genres of writing—marketing copy, journalism, speech writing, ghostwriting, food writing, etc. I wanted to find a landing spot for myself where I could think of writing not as the production of finished ideas but as a sandbox for working out thought, for allowing ideas to remain in play, where judgment could be suspended in favor of weighing ideas. I wanted writing to be a form of brainstorming, of posing questions rather than asserting answers. But after five years, during which my most public forms of address were fluff pieces for the *Wall Street Journal*, entries in my food blog, and Facebook posts, I was ready for something more urgent. Art criticism was not an obvious place to land, given what I wanted from writing—though there are many ways to be an art critic, many voices one can take, "judgment" is baked into the form—but it was a place where I could work out ideas.

In turning to art criticism during a period of online activism (which itself might be a contradiction in terms), and after having rejected my own academic complacency, I was determined to take seriously the lessons I had learned from reading Coates's "The Case for Reparations"—that after generations of stripping wealth and power (and therefore education and health and jobs and security and freedoms) from Black Americans, "equality" was not a sufficient response—justice would involve, at least in part, repayment *with interest*. Always a sucker for analogizing, I began to think of this concept beyond the limits of the monetary, using it as a basis for trying to imagine what a reparative mode of criticism could be. I should insist now that my imagining is just that; I don't think I've achieved it. But I know what I strive for. This is what I came up with.

First, how to make up for my own past inadequacies when it came to historicizing contemporary art? That would involve more than just paying attention to art practices and art histories I had previously overlooked (or, when I didn't overlook them, had framed in ways that did nothing to disrupt the overriding whiteness of my historical narrative). It did not mean, in other words, giving Black artists and artists of color equal time as of this moment forward—it meant *centering* the work of those artists in my writing.

Second, since I was now delving into writing about art that I had, because of my own failures of curiosity and education, little context for, I would have to abdicate any position of authority or judgment (the traditional voice of the art critic) and write as a student. That meant, for me, putting most of my effort into understanding the work on its own terms—educating myself, listening, and contributing to an art world filled with thinkers and makers who are conversing about Blackness.

Third—and this goes along with assuming the position of a student and writing about things that I don't yet know enough about in order to learn from them—I would learn how to talk about my own failures as part of my practice. I want to be an object lesson, the subject of a grown-up after-school special: learn from my mistakes.

I am convinced that our culture is weakened by people's inability to admit when they've done something wrong, when they've hurt someone, or when they've failed.

I had to put this third commitment to the test in the wake of the Jimmie Durham show, which I reviewed for *4Columns* during its run at the Hammer Museum. The text was my first about the work of a Native American artist. I relied on the show and the catalogue, including an essay by the excellent curator Paul Chaat Smith, to frame not only the art but the controversy surrounding it—a controversy that had to do with a question of whether the artist's implied claims of Cherokee heritage were true, and, if not, how to think about his art, which seems impossible to separate from that claimed identity. When the show moved to the Walker Art Center, long-rumbling protests by Cherokee curators and scholars to what they saw as Durham's misrepresentation of his status gained traction. In a Facebook group called Binder Full of People of Color in the Art World that I had begun in a fit of pique in 2015, when a white *New York Times* art critic lamented that there were no people of color in the art world, a heated discussion ensued on the issue of Durham's identity claims, and on questions of how or whether to reframe his art practice in light of the challenges to those claims. I had already gone on record praising the show and downplaying the rumblings, which led me to take the not so great but perhaps not surprising position of defending him so as to justify or excuse my own recently stated critical position. I found myself with plenty of company—I was but one of the scores of non–Native American art worlders who had suddenly become experts on tribal affiliation, blood quantum, and so on, based on five minutes of googling in the heat of a Facebook argument.

But thanks to the many members of that Facebook group coming from different Indigenous communities and affiliations who patiently but firmly explained the issues, I realized that my role as an art critic should not be to adjudicate Jimmie Durham's right to claim himself as Cherokee—that was, to say the least, not my business to decide—but to examine my own resistance to entertaining the possibility that this canonical artist might not belong in the canon. Criticism, in this case, meant something different than assessing whether artwork was good or bad, interesting or not—it meant examining the investments and limits of art criticism itself, which, in this case, were inseparable from the investments and limits of the art critic herself.

When I published the piece—"Mourning Jimmie Durham," which took as its conceit the seven stages of grief involved in reframing one's personal history of art—I was surprised when, on a Facebook thread, someone called me hypocritical for first praising the work and then, after the protests became louder, stepping back from that praise. This person saw my willingness to change my mind as a sign of my refusal to take a firm stand, of my inability to stick to my convictions. I understand why it might be understood that way—art critics are often expected to assess work from a position that is above the capricious ebbs and flows of momentary debate, especially in the outrage-fueled spaces of social media. One risks being misunderstood—changing one's mind, learning from one's mistakes, making one's mea culpas, or admitting one's biases is easily seen as hopping on the latest bandwagon, throwing one's lot in with the mob, blowing in the wind. That's okay. The willingness of art critics (and anyone, for that matter) to revisit their failures and be transparent about the evolution of their thinking is crucial in transforming how we write and think about art, and who we center as both our subjects and our audience.

Fourth, a reparative writing practice would require not just focusing on different subjects, but also writing for a different audience. We are often trained to assume a generic reader—at best, something like, "someone intelligent and informed but who reads at a sixth-grade level and is not a specialist about art," and at worst, "someone who has read the top twenty theory texts on my reading list." But I know that if I had ever thought of the race of that reader (and I'm sure I never did), I would have to admit that I assumed they were white—so well trained in the workings of white supremacy was I that, even as a brown person, I imagined that my default audience didn't look like me.

I have spent my whole life, in other words, reading art writing that was penned for a white gaze, and creating it myself. In the process, I erased my own subjectivity, along with that of others. So what would happen, I thought, if I tried to write with the assumption of a shared knowledge of certain concepts, like the existence of structural racism, or the phenomenon of white fragility, or the weaponized use of white tears, instead of feeling obligated to justify my use of such well-established analytical frameworks? What would happen if it were the responsibility of readers not familiar with my language to get up to speed—and not mine, as a subaltern voice, to translate myself? Would it turn cultural competency into an expectation for readers of art publications, the way knowledge of the esoteric thinking behind Minimalism or the basics of Greenbergian art criticism is treated as an expectation? Would it make space for other writers who shared my language to speak freely?

Fifth, across my practice as a whole, I would try to combine the two things that I love most—the close read, the nuanced description of the things I see when I look at an artwork, *and* the bird's-eye view of the institutions, power structures, and systems which frame everything we do as artists, curators, critics, historians, and viewers. I would write with the conviction that aesthetic understanding is inextricable from structural understanding, political understanding, economic and social understanding. My book *Whitewalling* is a foray into art criticism that doesn't analyze a single work of art—that asserts, among many arguments, a claim that we cannot see outside these determining factors, and that any claim to the contrary is suspect.

Now, once again: these are my goals, not my achievements. It is an ongoing challenge to unlearn the ways that I have been trained—both formally and informally—to see, think, and exist in the world. In setting these goals, I have and will continue to get it wrong; I have and will be called out for it when it happens. I have learned that the fear of being canceled weighs on me less heavily than the fear of writing in a manner that reinforces anti-Blackness and other forms of oppression. So I listen to the criticism and try to do better. And yes, I have been criticized—a lot. I don't worry so much about the criticism from within spaces of power, but I do take very seriously the words I hear from Black artists, critics, and students, or anyone who comes into contact with my work and is conscious of the ways in which my work might make their work harder, rather than easier.

I continue searching for a voice that I feel is adequate for this terrible and terrifying world, one filled with injustice and the everyday violence of anti-Blackness by state and citizen alike. I suppose I'll consider my own reparative writing practice successful when my voice, and the voices of other white and relatively privileged non-Black writers, becomes less important, and as other writers, so long barred from the major platforms where art criticism thrives, take over. I work for my own obsolescence, and until then, I work to hold space for a different kind of art world.

This article was adapted from a talk by Aruna D'Souza, "Writing in the Reparative Mode," an AICA-USA Distinguished Critic Lecture in partnership with the Vera List Center for Art and Politics, presented at the New School, November 26, 2018.

MIRA DAYAL: Art criticism often upholds "critical distance"—in theory, being farther from the work gives you more of a vantage point onto the work, or more territory from which to be critical. But all of you in some way allude to a community that is associated with your writing, or note how the language you're using is associated with a particular community. How do you negotiate that supposed critical distance, or desire for critical distance, and your own proximity to a community of artists and writers that you want to align yourself with or that you are already part of?

AMY FUNG: Critical distance doesn't work for me. I like to write in an honest way about things that are close to me, that I care about. Writing critically about a work that you want to be better is a generous act that I don't want to throw away on people who don't want to hear it. My sense of community has really been shifting since I actively said I was leaving the art world. You really see who your friends are. I care about people who have good boundaries and people who are doing the work of self-interrogation. That group often falls within queer, POC communities because we have to do that work. Nobody's doing it for us.

MD: And do you see your writing as the primary way in which you self-interrogate?

AF: The book that I just published, *Before I Was a Critic, I Was a Human Being*, is 100 percent self-interrogation.

MD: In some ways, it's a self-portrait or autobiography, and in some ways it's a land acknowledgment, but there is no place in the book where it feels like an art review.

AF: Art criticism also tells you about the critic. Much of historic art criticism shows you that it was written by white males who didn't have to hide their biases against works that they didn't understand, that they couldn't see themselves in. I wanted to show where I was coming from. Looking back at what I've written, I'm not being an asshole because I don't like your modernist, apolitical work. I'm saying that it takes a lot of privilege for you to make it.

REAL LIFE V. *ART CRITICISM*: A META-ART CASE STUDY

ANA TUAZON

In a pre-internet New York City, an exciting publishing ecosystem flourished among communities of artists. Hyper-local coverage emerged via personal newsletters, artist-run journals, and even the more traditional newspapers and magazines, which had a more robust neighborhood-level presence. This was a culture of publishing that affirmed the inherent value of public discourse in a way that seems lost today, though publishing now happens constantly via the internet. Particularly striking is how correspondence functioned: rather than being limited to the "personal" sphere, it served as a public vehicle for critique (now, comments sections on online articles provide an illusion of this dynamic, but they can't begin to compare). Reader responses, disagreements, conflicts, and even bitter take-downs were given space on the page in ways that seem unimaginable today; letters to editors and open letters were particularly powerful tools to call for change. In 1978, a letter from the Combahee River Collective to the mostly white editors of *Heresies* caused the feminist journal to reform its editorial approach and allow women artists of color more agency. The Godzilla Asian American Arts Network published an open letter in 1991 protesting the exclusion of Asian artists from the Whitney Biennial, spurring the museum to show work by one of their members and hire another as curator. Letters made a subjective and collective voice of critique possible.

There is a weirder, messier example of correspondence between an artist and a critic that I also find meaningful—Adrian Piper's "An Open Letter to Donald Kuspit," published in the winter 1987 volume of the artist-run magazine *Real Life*. The conflict between Piper and Kuspit centers on an essay by the latter writer that had originally been commissioned on the occasion of Piper's Alternative Museum exhibition "Reflections: 1967–1987." Strangely, Kuspit saw this as an opportunity to air disparaging and at times misogynistic opinions about her work, leading Piper to reject the text from the catalogue—but Kuspit escalated the situation by publishing his essay in the journal *Art Criticism,* of which he was an editor. Kuspit's essay psychoanalyzes Piper almost as if she were his patient, arguing that her hyper-discursive approach to self-representation, her "talkative performance of herself," arrives from a pathologically insecure, narcissistic personality. He labels her "the proverbial snake that has taken its tail in its mouth—indeed, one can say the bite of self-articulation is her act of art—and become a cosmos complete unto itself."

In contrast, Piper's response approaches Kuspit as a (former) friend, publishing the private correspondence she'd sent about the essay before it was printed in *Art Criticism*. She addresses him as "Donald" and, in drawings accompanying the letter, illustrates versions of some of the violent fantasies that Kuspit seemed to project onto her. In one, Kuspit is depicted as a scowling cockroach, while the other shows Piper under attack, with Kuspit's words jumping off a page and forming snakes that coil violently around her neck. A nearby canister labeled meta art threatens to spray deadly fumes.

I bring up this example not necessarily to glorify public feuds, but to highlight the importance of publishing spaces that allow (or even encourage) talking back. Piper deserves to be recognized as a vital author of this form of criticism, which intersects with the rhetoric of protest, or *complaint*, that Sara Ahmed has theorized as a touchstone of feminist pedagogy.

Why was *Real Life* a platform for such antagonistic discourse? The project, funded by an NEA grant, is described in a Primary Information anthology as an informal record of the "art, influences, and preoccupations of a loose clique of artworld figures of the Eighties," and particularly "material that was ignored by established art magazines at the time." Some of that material is narrowly focused and no longer seems urgent, but as a rare collection of criticism by artists, it's interesting to consider, and its pages contain a real sense of unfolding conversation, of theories being tested and risks taken. In the current political climate, funding for such offbeat projects is scarce, which correlates with a more risk-averse publishing culture. *Real Life*'s approach is in step with Piper's "meta-art" model (outlined in a 1973 essay in *Artforum*, and impugned within Kuspit's critique), in which artists "stand off and view our role of artist reflectively; that we see the fact of our art-making as itself a discrete state or process with interesting implications worthy of pursuing; that we articulate and present these implications to an audience (either the same as or broader than the art audience) for comment, evaluation, and feedback."

Meta-art imagines a world in which an artist's voice contributes to the production of meaning just as much as the work they display, and calls for artists to depart from the idea of a practice confined to the studio in favor of a holistic, public-facing approach to making. We could imagine that under this model, the traditional distinctions between artist, critic, and audience are more mutable, as are the hierarchies attached to these relationships. Piper's open letter takes this idea to an extreme, but her commitment to the performance allows us to see the absurd violence of Kuspit's power play (which ironically displays the same insecure self-importance he accuses her of). Self-articulation is here both an expression of vulnerability and a protest against intellectual domination.

LESLIE DICK: One of the questions you asked, which I think is a really interesting one, is who are you writing for when you write? Who are you writing alongside? What is your scene of writing? Who is it addressed to?

ANNIE GODFREY LARMON: One of the big differences here, between studio critiques and art reviews, is duration. In the MFA environment, in the workshop environment, there's time, there's space, there's reaction, which is also not simply textual. So many elements enter that environment, but it's a completely different form. A 600-word review has very specific parameters, and if you're lucky, you know to a certain degree who your audience is because a few people might respond to you. You brought up Aruna D'Souza's lecture from earlier this year where she talks about a model of reparations through criticism, which I thought was really interesting and shifted the address of the assumed audience to one that is potentially not who's typically addressed—writing for an audience who you don't assume has been keeping up on *October*, or who doesn't have a degree in critical theory and art history, or who has a different set of references, or who is ultimately more generous to people who have been marginalized by the leading elitist critical discourse—that's really interesting to me.

I mean, personally, when I was thinking about your question, I think I honestly write to the artist. I find a lot of sympathy with the Baudelaire quote that *4Columns* has mobilized as its mission statement—to write from an exclusive point of view, but one which opens a work to its broadest horizons. I think, as Aruna suggests, for me the project of criticism is trying to access many interpretations of this object's terms: What is the matter at hand with an object? Sometimes an identity is relevant, sometimes it is not. To what degree have the conditions of its display, or institutions or galleries, made it possible for me to see this work? I try to consider all of these factors as I'm developing a piece. I try to be very generous, which I think a lot of people would really disagree with because it questions the critical function. But from where I'm coming from, the kind of criticism that I want to write or the kind of art writing—maybe we don't even call it criticism in a way, it's sort of a critique reconceived along this idea of productive conflict.

MIRA DAYAL: Both of you used the term "resource" at different points in your writing. Who are we allocating this resource to?

LESLIE DICK: I feel the resource is, in the art school context, for anyone in the room who is an artist. Everyone has an interest in learning how to think and talk about artwork, especially when it's not your own. You can actually nourish your own practice as you measure the difference between the way you approach making a sculpture and this other sculpture that's in the room with us.

I'm a very idea-driven person, so I get incredible joy out of ideas, and I see artworks—and a lot of artists would disagree with me—as mechanisms for generating ideas. They're chugging away, like a generator, and my task is to understand not only what's coming out, but also how the mechanism is operating to make that idea available to me. And then someone else in the conversation can say, "No, I don't agree. The green underneath is not signifying nature. The green signifies separation, and death." Neither of us has to be right. But to me there's a resource in simply allowing for the space of uncertainty. I say to my students, I'm not interested in you graduating from CalArts and having success and being picked up by a gallery right away. What I'm interested in is you still making art twenty years from now. I want you to be able to recall and revive this kind of critical conversation on your own, when you're going to your studio ten or twenty years from now. Some of this energy will be available to you because it's—I use the word generative. It's action. It's not information. It's process. It's engagement, and it's collectivity, and it's community.

CORRECTING COURSE: READING A REFRAMED CANON

ERICA CARDWELL

Agendas can work in different ways, particularly if the framing involves race. As a Black woman, with regard to writing and teaching, I often consider how my identity, context, and politics shape how I, my students, or readers respond to the world. I am also conscious of how, through my work as a critic and as a teacher, I can counter the expectations and canons of the field.

These questions were clearly illustrated in one of my first-year English composition classes. Prior to joining academia, I had primarily taught in community-based, nonprofit settings with groups of mostly young Black and brown people. Therefore, I was accustomed to developing reading lists and syllabi that reflected those young people's identities and concerns. For this class, my syllabus contained authors such as Ta-Nehisi Coates, Langston Hughes, Amy Tan, Gloria Anzaldúa, Malcolm X, Jamaica Kincaid, Malcolm Gladwell, George Orwell, and Maya Angelou. At this school, the white students were in the minority; most of the students were Latinx, Black, South and East Asian. A young white man, who was a former Marine finishing his degree under the GI Bill, claimed concern about the predominance of Black authors in my syllabus. As the only white student in my class, he stood out—yet he always sat in the front row and contributed confidently to our discussions. I only learned of his opposition later, from the white female tenured faculty member who was conducting my routine observation. The morning of the observation, the professor sat along the wall of the classroom quietly taking notes. I could see him eyeing her. By the end of class, he approached her, and they stepped outside to talk.

A day or two later, I received my observation notes. In the comments section, she shared that a student had approached her after class "expressing concern that there were mostly Black authors on the syllabus." From my tiny wooden desk in the bedroom of my Queens apartment, I re-read the paragraph several times. I wasn't sure if her tone was one of derision or simply reporting what had occurred. I slid away from my desk and started firing off text messages to my friend, a white queer woman who was teaching English while finishing her PhD; occasionally, we would ply ourselves with cheap whiskey and even cheaper cigarettes at a dark dive bar in our neighborhood, parsing our woes. I reached out to her deliberately, not only because she was a queer colleague and adjunct comrade currently teaching a similar class, but also recognizing that, as a white woman, she may be able to advise me on the best way to both retaliate and protect myself in this situation.

Before we met, I prepared a rant about the angst of being observed despite being paid extraordinarily low wages. I was ready to commiserate about the sense of betrayal I felt from that student, who, despite his congenial presence, had perceived the observing professor's role as one of authority—and decided to confide in her instead.

To my surprise, this friend presented me with a whole other framing. When she saw my somber face, she reminded me that I had not done anything wrong. She asked if the observer had redirected the student, clarifying that it was her job to support me. This perspective initially bewildered me. I hadn't realized that I could *expect* the observer's support, rather than make the case for it.

What I came to realize is that everyone in this scenario was operating with their own agenda, a mode of functioning to obtain a specific result. The student had taken issue with the fact that the academic standards he'd been raised around—the presence of mostly white authors on a syllabus—weren't being upheld, and with this agenda of preserving the canon, he took solace in expressing his concern to a white female professor despite our previously collegial relationship. My agenda—unabashed and unwavering—has always been aimed at disrupting the canon and offering as many opportunities as possible for my students of color to recognize themselves in the assigned readings, and for non-POC students to experience a more expansive literary world. The academy would like us to believe that the observer's role is to ensure that the instruction follows suitable and appropriate standards for the school and students. While I found my observer to be impartial, I also found her approach aligned with her position of power, as she delivered this feedback with little context.

At the time, the most confusing aspect of the situation was that my power had always been under scrutiny, and according to the student, it was not my place to suggest that things could be done differently. Did this student think that by incorporating Black authors into a class on literature, I would shift the conversation into a discussion of race? Did this student believe that race and literature could be separated? Or did he believe that he would lose a universal connection if he was asked to read and experience the work of authors who didn't look like him?

When I met with the observer, I asked her if she had mentioned to him that his comment could have been addressed directly to me. She confirmed that she had, and added, "They get uncomfortable, don't they? When they have to experience things out of their comfort zone." Per her suggestion, I put out a mid-semester survey to the class, to give students the opportunity to anonymously disclose their impressions of the course, syllabus, assignments, etc., thus far. As I handed out the survey, the student's eyes widened, and he directed his focus down to the paper in front of him. Many of the students reported that they enjoyed the readings and were pleased to have been introduced to authors they had never heard of before. Some students mentioned that they were relieved to finally be able to relate to the assigned readings, while others felt overwhelmed by the volume. The student in question spoke little throughout the rest of the semester, but still completed his assignments in a diligent and timely fashion.

Since then, my composition syllabi have evolved. I will often begin the semester with collaborative agreements orienting the students to my canonical approach. Not an agenda per se, but more of a shared intention. The aim is to introduce norm-busting from the very beginning. And depending on whether the course is a requirement or one focused on self-selected interests, I explicitly state that the selection of course material is my pedagogical choice, meant to ensure a well-rounded classroom experience, further empowering students to make decisions based on their own needs, and agendas.

As a critic, I find it crucial to announce my terms in a similar way. My writing prioritizes artists of color, countering their broader cultural absence by reimagining the archive and deconstructing the thorny power dynamics I faced in my classroom. My objective is to correct course, not to abnegate work made by non-POC artists, many of whom I greatly admire and have learned from. This agenda is a political reframing, a close read that raises the question: How do our perceptions and perspectives shift when our points of reference are more inclusive? While the moment in my classroom was incredibly isolating, it also signaled a clear and decisive way forward despite potential hostility. To dismiss my approach stifles the vital elements of contemporary criticism—passionate, curious inquiry always in favor of and fascination with discourse in service of the commons.

CONTRIBUTOR BIOS

KEMI ADEYEMI

I began writing with and about artists as a PhD student in Northwestern's Department of Performance Studies. Since then, my relationship to art criticism has been entirely shaped by the generosity of the artists, curators, and culture workers who have invited me to think with them. I direct the Black Embodiments Studio (Seattle, WA) in an effort to return the favor, providing space where people can develop complex and creative conversations around race and aesthetics.

ELISA WOUK ALMINO

My first love was writing; then came my passion for visual art. I wanted to explore writing about art in a more accessible, personable way, so I went down the journalistic route, as opposed to the academic one. My first published pieces weren't about art, though. While working as a fact-checker at the *Nation*, I contributed a short piece about Brazil's prison problem; I was also becoming interested in literary translation and wrote my first book reviews, about Antonio Tabucchi and Guillermo Rosales in English translation, for *Words Without Borders*. Writing for magazines, and then getting a degree in cultural journalism, helped me let go of my "college voice" and start finding my own. This was much harder than I thought it would be, and I am grateful to all the editors and professors who pushed me to be clear and direct in my writing. Those shifts also helped me in my work as an editor at *Hyperallergic*, and now at the *Los Angeles Times*, and in my translations of Brazilian poets like Ana Martins Marques, Paulo Leminski, and Ana Cristina Cesar. Over the years, I've increasingly focused on writing about art that engages with themes of home, belonging, and displacement, in part because of my experience as a Brazilian who has lived outside of Brazil for most of my life. Today I see my roles as a writer, editor, and translator as deeply intertwined and I can't imagine doing one without the others.

ANDY CAMPBELL

My first pieces of art criticism/journalism were written for the *Austin Chronicle*, an independent alternative news weekly, and were the result of striking up a friendship with Kate X Messer, one of the editors of the publication that was the holy grail of local journalism for me and my friends. I began as a blogger for the paper's "Gay Place," a hub for local/national LGBTQ community news and events, and aided in writing the yearly "Best of Austin" blurbs (still some of the most fun writing I've ever done). Messer also taught me how to DJ, and we would play at gay bars and queer-ish events around town as "DJs Fine and Dandy with Kate and Andy."

Eventually, I was introduced to the arts editor at the *Austin Chronicle* and began to write more formal reviews and short studio interviews with Austin-area artists. Being a member of a larger community of artists was always important to me, and the studio visit interviews were an opportunity to get some insight into artistic practice and share this with a broader Austin readership. Around that same time, Lauren O'Neill Butler, who was then an editor at *Artforum*, presented a series of lectures at the University of Texas at Austin, where I was a graduate student in art history. After a brief meeting during one of her visits, she offered me the opportunity to write some short reviews for *Artforum* online. I wrote my first review for that publication (on Catherine Opie's photographs) while on a visit to Boston, helping a lesbian couple get pregnant as a known sperm donor.

A review is never a throwaway piece of writing for me, but a chance to reassess and learn anew: to rescript (and sometimes reaffirm) the way I see. Review writing, and short-form writing in general, is like working a familiar yet often-ignored muscle, perhaps one of those stretchy ones in your neck that you wouldn't be able to name. Even now, as a professor in the context of an art school, I find that writing reviews is one of the exercises keeping my head on, grounding me in my wider writing practice (which includes longer, more academic, and more experimental modes), turning my attention this way and that, keeping me limber and aware.

ERICA CARDWELL

Around 2008, I started writing personal essays about Black visual culture. These essays were often lacking in canonical or traditional vocabulary, and instead focused more on storytelling and themes of race and gender. An early essay called "Myriad Selves" examined the grid-like pattern of repetition in Mark Bradford's *Jheri Now, Curl Later* (2001) as a symbol for the roving aftermath of my mother's sudden death and my emerging queer identity.

In 2015, one of my first reviews was published. It was an essay comparing a massive, crowd-pleasing Basquiat retrospective at the Art Gallery of Ontario (AGO) in Toronto—the first exhibition of his work in Canada—to an exhibition of Basquiat's notebooks at the Brooklyn Museum. The latter show exposed Basquiat's intimate thoughts as a Black male artist beyond the youthful, fame-seeking persona he became known for. I was writing against the backdrop of the death of Freddie Gray, the young Black teenager who died while in Baltimore police custody. I discussed the AGO exhibition's use of sensationalized sound bites and mass-produced souvenirs to draw in large crowds alongside the Brooklyn Museum's opportunities for more intimate processing of the artist's personal reflections. My central question concerned the ethical tension in featuring Basquiat's private notebooks as a fraught justification for his humanity and the symbolic life and work of a Black male artist in a predominantly white art world. I asked, did Basquiat's desire for fame preclude his right to privacy? In the essay, I looked at my own compulsive journaling habit and briefly considered the invasiveness of ever having them on display, even after I'm gone.

Now, as a writer and teacher, I ask my students to mine their own consciousness; I require daily journal writing and ask them to read aloud their own work. Repetition, like the grid, is an essential component of my pedagogical approach. The prompt I have worked with most recently asks students to "earn the I." This prompt leans away from production and toward attentiveness to invoke a sense of intimacy without fear. What does the art require from me? How does the writer engage vulnerably on the page in service of the art?

DESSANE LOPEZ CASSELL

As a kid, I dreamt of writing novels or becoming a painter. My dual interests in art and writing (and apparent love of uphill battles) led me to study art history as an undergrad. While I currently hold the fancy title of Editor-in-Chief at *Seen* journal, I spent my early twenties working in museums and arts nonprofits, all the while holding down a slew of secondary positions to help pay the bills. Dismayed by the mainstream art world's lack of imagination, I eventually started writing and curating independently, which gave me the space to learn about artists and filmmakers whose voices had long been omitted from museum collections. So while my first bylines were in museum catalogues, I'd credit the qualities I rely on most as a writer—thick skin, empathy, and the ability to patiently observe—to the years I spent working my second shift in bars and restaurants.

RE'AL CHRISTIAN

There are two essays I return to as a writer: "Salvation" by Langston Hughes, from his autobiography *The Big Sea*, and "On Self-Respect" by Joan Didion, from *Slouching Toward Bethlehem*. I initially read these texts during my first year of college. I had never realized how personal, intimate, and vulnerable writing could be, and how that vulnerability could inspire others to share their own histories—no matter how distressing, embarrassing, or esoteric. I had an artistic practice when I was in high school, but as much as I loved making art, I was more drawn to speaking and writing about it. I was interested in the precision of language, not as an alternative to visual art, but as a new medium to explore. The first publication I wrote for was *Art Versed*, where I was introduced to the process of working with an editor, something that I think is underemphasized in the classroom.

My mentor, Kenneth E. Silver, encouraged my writing when I was his student at New York University. He taught me his approach to art writing: how to tell a story, build a world around the art itself. He also gave me my first foothold in the field. A few years after I graduated, he introduced me to the editor of *Art in America*, who also happened to be his former student. This wasn't something I asked for, so I was all the more grateful for his generosity.

Building relationships with mentors takes time, care, and mutual respect. My experience with *Art in America* instilled an important lesson that I've carried with me—the importance of knowing how to ask for something I want—but equally important is recognizing the dedication it takes to be a writer. While this opportunity opened a door, I've come across other boundaries that many writers face. This profession is often romanticized, but it demands endurance, daily rhythm, intellectual and emotional labor (with the right mix of humility and self-respect). I find mentorship in writers like James Baldwin, bell hooks, and Toni Morrison, not only for the singular elegance of their words, but also for the ways in which they speak to the very occupation of being a Black writer, in all its nuance, frustration, joy, rage, and beauty.

ARUNA D'SOUZA

After leaving my career as an academic art historian in 2012, I sought to "retrain" myself as a writer (and pay my bills; I was a single mom) by plunging into a variety of genres, including food writing, corporate writing, speech writing, social media writing, and journalism. I only turned back to art writing in 2016, when a friend of mine, Margaret Sundell, said she was starting *4Columns*, an online magazine devoted to criticism in the arts, and asked me to become a regular contributor. I had known Margaret since grad school, but was thrilled that she was interested in having me write for her not because of my former art historical writing but because of my food blog—in other words, she valued where I wanted to go in my work, not where I had come from. Under her tutelage—I've never had any formal training as a writer, and Margaret is a formidable and talented editor—I began to develop my skills. The next year, the artist Paul Chan asked me to do the impossible: write a book about the 2017 Whitney Biennial controversy quickly enough that it could be published while the issue was still on people's minds. *Whitewalling: Art, Race, and Protest in 3 Acts* came out exactly a year after the 2017 biennial opened; to achieve that timing, I wrote it in two months. That experience, too, was an education—this time in efficiency and getting over my ego because I simply didn't have time to fuss about it.

Both of these opportunities—*4Columns* and *Whitewalling*—and indeed the vast majority of my professional gigs, came about because of my presence on social media. In the fall of 2022, I took a position as WW Corcoran Visiting Professor of Social Engagement at the Corcoran School of Art: the invitation had come via Facebook Messenger, and the person who invited me told me she wanted me to "do in the classroom what I do online." In April 2022, I had deleted my Facebook and Twitter accounts because of my frustration at the increasingly undeniable evilness of both platforms; whether this will have an effect on my career is yet to be seen. In the meantime, I continue writing for *4Columns*, and for the *New York Times*, as well as for a lot of other publications, galleries, and museums, because the truth is that as a freelancer you have to write a whole lot to keep your head above water financially.

LESLIE DICK

I started writing short pieces on contemporary art because I was thrilled by the challenge of bringing words to objects and events that seemed indescribable. This writing appeared in tiny print magazines and catalogues. Later, I was encouraged by a friend, Eli Pulsinelli, who prodded me to write about an Eva Hesse show and traveled with me to see it. Her conviction that I had something valuable to say was crucial. Teaching at CalArts for almost thirty years clarified my practice: I see my role as articulating, in language, the ways that artworks operate as mechanisms for generating meaning. As a member of the editorial board at *X-TRA*, I work closely with different writers, with the intention of bringing out all the possibilities in their writing.

AMY FUNG
Having very little clue how traditional print publishing worked, I began freelance writing by sending in a fully written and unsolicited piece of music criticism to a local and now defunct weekly (*ed magazine*) straight out of high school. (The piece was accepted, with a warning to never do that again.) After a few years of intermittent writing about arts and culture in a nondescript Canadian city for another weekly (*See Magazine*), I started a blog in the mid-aughts to house my critical art reviews, which, at that point, my editor had vehemently told me nobody wanted. Not about their friends. Not about themselves. No one wanted criticism. Eventually my new writings were embraced by a competing publication (*Vue Weekly*) as a print column, and I soon began writing for national (*C Magazine, Canadian Art*) and international (*Frieze, Art Papers*) publications. When my freelance writing began to take off, I was stably employed at a corporate magazine publishing house, where I learned about the basic tenets of direct marketing, the dying art of circulation, and the confusion about and resistance to online publishing that have since plagued the majority of publications still remaining. Eventually, I returned to writing as a creative practice. My first book, *Before I Was a Critic I Was a Human Being*, was published in 2019 by Book*hug Press and Artspeak, and is not really about art at all.

MERRAY GERGES
I studied art history at the Nova Scotia College of Art and Design and journalism at King's University in Halifax, where I cofounded and coedited *CRIT*, a free biannual criticism publication. I held various editorial positions at *Canadian Art* from 2016 to 2019. From 2019 to 2020, I was the inaugural editorial fellow at *C Magazine*, where I produced three print issues addressing facets of systemic change. My writing has appeared in *Momus*, *Hyperallergic*, the Gardiner Museum blog, Esker Foundation, and other publications, where I have tended to pay more attention to art's contexts rather than its contents. I am currently working on a new body of long-form essays after completing an MFA in narrative nonfiction at New York University's journalism school.

ARIEL GOLDBERG
I envision art writing that resembles moving through an exhibition with a friend and articulating the thoughts and questions, arguments and discussions that arise in the process

of describing and trying to understand the work. I started art writing probably out of a naive fascination with Susan Sontag. I was drawn to answer the provocation of encountering art and feeling myself to be in dialogue with artworks. I self-published at first and distributed writings to those I shared creative spaces with. Grassroots spaces and artist-run event series are where I first aired my writing that could be called art criticism, often as short texts read out loud. I first published my nonfiction with Nightboat Books in 2016. I was working at the time as a readings coordinator at the Poetry Project and this put me in direct conversation with writers and artists and audiences: very alive situations. I considered my introductions at each event to be short pieces of art criticism.

I studied writing at universities, but I learned much more figuring things out on my own, by reading widely, drafting and sharing texts with my best friend, Jess Barbagallo, and with other close friends. My lovers have been my most honest editors; I am indebted to them. I miss the columns that artists used to have in magazines where it was more like a public diary and art writers were supported to focus on their writing. I have been very grateful for the opportunities to publish in *Art in America*, *Artforum*, and *e-flux*, but when you are writing for the broader art world, the editing process is so extensive. I am not a fast writer, so these assignments take me a long time. Writing for a poetry press gave me a certain degree of freedom to embrace what some consider the marginal in both content and form. I am interested in art writing that is perhaps not trying to be fast. As I write on photography (beyond ubiquitous) and trans and queer life which has sustained itself far from mainstream art establishments, my biggest sources of inspiration are oral histories and the slow work of talking to the culture workers, artists, and documentarians whose work I am in conversation with. Process is my favorite part of the process.

YVES JEFFCOAT

I became interested in art criticism when I realized that it was a meaningful and accessible way to explore topics and concepts that I care about: critical thought and conversation, learning about and engaging with art, and crafting narratives to share ideas and shift perceptions. I nurtured my interest in the field by participating in an art writing mentorship program at *Burnaway*, the publication where I previously interned and where I first published my art criticism. Today my interests in yoga, social change, and storytelling inform my writing.

DANA KOPEL

I started writing more regularly about art while I was in grad school for curating. In addition to my coursework, I published exhibition reviews in *Modern Painters*, where my editor, Thea Ballard, was an acquaintance who eventually became a coworker at the New Museum and a dear friend. I wrote about a variety of exhibitions but was particularly interested in those that engaged questions of gender, sexuality, and materiality. As I got involved in organizing the New Museum Union, my interests within art criticism shifted; I'm now most invested in writing about labor in the cultural sector—including museum worker organizing, artists who deal explicitly with work, and the art world's recent political upheavals. I used to see my writing as participation in a discourse and in a series of networks; while that's still true to an extent, I'm increasingly interested in thinking about it as propaganda.

ANNIE GODFREY LARMON

I started writing art criticism for an independent weekly in Portland, Maine, where I was curating projects and interested in generating critical discourse around regionalist work. I received a fellowship from the Andy Warhol Foundation to work with *Artforum*'s Alex Scrimgeour, who introduced me to the pleasures of the editorial dialectic, just as I entered the Center for Curatorial Studies at Bard College. There, I took an excellent art writing course with another *Artforum* editor, the inimitable Elizabeth Schambelan, who expanded my sense of what criticism made possible, not only in terms of assessing work according to its many contexts—its audience, historical precedence, systems of value, function—but also in terms of form, voice, and play. I soon started writing for *Frieze*, *Artforum*, and *MAY*, and then joined *Artforum* as International Reviews Editor.

I tend to write about artists who represent, attend to, or challenge the impact technology has on language, bodies, labor, and subjectivity; and I prefer to write about underrepresented artists and those who have been historically overlooked. The writing itself equally relies on the generosity of the editors I work with—who negotiate the mechanics of a text and distill arguments—and the freer, imprecise, and sometimes crackpot space of experimentation and association in conversations with friends. As an editor, I have worked on books for MOMA PS1, Lévy Gorvy, and the Hessel Museum of Art. I am now based in Garrison, New York, where I am at work on my first novel.

YANIYA LEE

I was raised by Black women artists, and while I always wanted to write fiction, I was daunted by the task. I started writing about art to engage critically with artists and learn the visual languages they used to share their perspectives on the world. My first pieces were for my local weekly arts and culture magazine, the *Montreal Mirror*. I pitched my editor every week and quickly developed relationships with the communications people at the local museums and galleries who would keep me informed on upcoming events and exhibitions.

Being able to work through undigested ideas with people I trusted and respected has always been helpful in getting from first messy draft to final polished edit. The blogs and weeklies I initially wrote for had minimal editorial support, so I found friends and colleagues who were familiar with my interests to talk through my writing.

I still see my writing as a conversation with a visual artist.

In addition to extensive research, interviews have always been an important part of how I come to an artist's work; all the thinking I do is an extension of that dialogue.

JESSICA LYNNE

More than a decade ago, my dear friend Ope Bukola created *Zora Magazine*, a digital publication for Black women writers. On a forum hosted by our alma mater, I recall reading one of Ope's posts that invited those interested in publishing, digital media, and Black women's writing to contact her and learn more about *Zora*. I responded, and not only did I begin a beautiful friendship, but I began to think more explicitly about who I was as a writer, who I wanted to be as a writer, and the possibilities therein. At *Zora*, we did not publish (nor did I write) art criticism per se, but this experience is crucial to my relationship to publishing more generally, and I'm glad to have the chance to name that experience as the pivotal foundation that it was. Without Ope's friendship and support, I would have never had the audacity to believe in myself, and with that youthful ambition, I might not have joined Taylor Aldridge in creating *ARTS.BLACK*.

Indeed, when *ARTS.BLACK* was founded, in 2014, I had not published much at all. Sometimes it is difficult to read the writings composed by my younger self. In them, I encounter a person trying to sort through her thoughts on art, culture, politics—getting too much wrong. But I suppose making mistakes, rethinking formerly held opinions, and recognizing it all later is part of what it means to be a writer and a reader, and to keep growing as a thinker. I owe so much to Taylor and Ope for their love. I later found support in working with brilliant writers and editors such as Jillian Steinhauer (who was one of my first editors during her time at *Hyperallergic*), Ben Davis, Cameron Shaw, Charlie Tatum, and poet/critic Claudia La Rocco. Along the way, *ARTS.BLACK* continued to serve as an editorial home for Black (art) critics, and I tried my best to navigate the murky terrain of art media while working day jobs and learning how to not burn out.

Some seven or eight years on, I have found myself burned out, appalled by the field's lip service towards Black (women) writers, and I am not sure that this is even the work I will be doing some seven or eight years from *now*. Still, I recognize that without foundations such as the Ford Foundation, Andy Warhol Foundation, and Graham Foundation for Advanced Studies in Fine Arts supporting me and *ARTS.BLACK*, I might have left this work years ago.

When people ask me what I do for a living, I tend to shrug and quietly respond, "art critic," though that does not always feel good or quite right. Art criticism is interesting, complicated, often surprising work, and if I come back to *this* text sometime in the future, and I am no longer a critic, I have decided that I will be fine with that. I want to write and read and think about culture and politics and art, and if what we know and understand to be art criticism is not the best container for that in the long term, then I think it is important to let that be my truth. I say this as a way of giving myself permission to remain elastic and playful as a writer. And I hope, for anyone reading this, it might be a way of giving them permission to evolve and change too.

ASHLEY STULL MEYERS

I am a writer, editor, and curator who received my first opportunities to publish as a graduate student while living in San Francisco. I owe my vision for humanizing arts discourse to my time as a part of the (now shuttered) *Art Practical* and *Daily Serving* communities of writers. My favorite publishing projects experiment with humor, vulnerability, and pop-cultural reference. I am inspired by artist magazines of the 1980s and 1990s, and the moments when the objecthood of a nice book and the practice of exhibition-making can come together. My work hopes to illustrate that art (and its affiliate language) has the power to make keen observers, comedians, and romantics of us all.

TAUSIF NOOR

I began writing about art for small online blogs and websites as a way to stave off a fear of regressing—intellectually, socially, emotionally—after undergrad. Writing art criticism for publications such as *Artforum*, *Frieze*, and *Momus* offered an escape from the drudgery of a brief, misguided entanglement with corporate America, and later an entry point for working in nonprofit art organizations and museums. Today, it complements and often functions as a reprieve from academic research and offers instructive ways to navigate institutionality. Through the support of mentors, editors, and friends and peers in the freelance trenches, writing has been a way to engage expansively with visual culture. People and their ideas, theories, and complications motivate me to continue as a critic. Writing is a lonely task, made lonelier by the dwindling possibilities of sustaining a life in the arts, but it is my hope that an idea, rippling out across space and time, might touch another life—however momentarily—and beget other, sturdier, more radical forms. I offer this: Given the condition that writing is only ever processual and never complete, so too is the person undertaking these tasks; therefore, eclecticism is the best and perhaps only mode of operation. Drawing as much from art history and contemporary image culture as from queer feminism, anti-colonial history, and Marxist philosophy, I have yoked myself to the modest goal of undoing the enterprise of criticism as unqualified appraisal.

KRISTINA KAY ROBINSON

My formal background is in literature. However, my critical and creative writing has always used visual texts as frameworks for cultural and character analysis. Some of my earlier essays for publications such as *Guernica* and the *Nation*, for example, are a mix of cultural, literary, and art criticism. My perspective as a literary fiction writer, poet, and cultural critic informs my approach to writing art criticism as it relates to syntax, voice, and style. I also have a practice as a visual artist that definitely shapes what I see as the role of criticism. I try to be an honest extension of the experience of the artwork as a critic, and a conduit for feeling as an artist. I believe I bring a belief in both freedom and dexterity to the discipline.

JILLIAN STEINHAUER

I studied some art history in college and started writing criticism when I met an editor for *NY Arts* magazine on a plane and convinced him to divulge his email address. The magazine put my first review on its cover. The first time I got paid for a piece of writing was several months later, in November 2007, when the *Village Voice* gave me $175 for a 350-word review. Soon after, I got hired as an editorial assistant at *Artinfo*—my first job in the field. I learned a lot about the art world there. At my most recent job—five years as an editor at *Hyperallergic*—I learned the ins and outs of editing as well as fast-paced reporting and blogging. But the place where I probably learned the most about the work I love to do was in grad school, in the cultural reporting and criticism program at NYU. I am in major debt because of it, but I have no regrets (yet). These days, I am highly critical of the art world, but I still care about art. I'm more politically and socially aware than I was at the start; I also move more slowly. I try to bring those socio-political perspectives to my work as a freelance critic and reporter for places like the *New York Times*, the *Nation*, and the *New Republic*. I often think of myself as an interpreter, demystifying contemporary art for a mainstream audience. I still struggle sometimes with the notion that my writing has more substance than style. Once a critic, always a critic, right?

ANA TUAZON

The nonprofit online publications *Daily Serving*, *Temporary Art Review*, and *Art Practical* all published me as a new writer, but they are no longer active. Those early, small successes were the foundation of my confidence as a critical writer; they were proof that space existed for me to speak publicly. Today I see how much harder it is to find these pathways in a landscape where independent arts media is perpetually devalued, while the boundary between editorial and advertising content grows blurrier. I also ask myself, is that a landscape in which I want to be successful?

I'm excited about the alternatives that keep reemerging, like newsletters and publishing collectives. I want us to invest more in the underground, an essential space for the kind of criticism that shapes and is shaped by collectively (rather than institutionally) held knowledge.

MONICA USZEROWICZ

I was born in Brooklyn to Ashkenazi-Jewish and Afro–Puerto Rican parents, grew up in Ft. Lauderdale, and now live in Miami. I've utilized writing to understand and respond to both my internal life and my connection to other people; I needed to make sense of my place in the world, or figure out if I had one. I was always going to write, even if no one was going to read it.

After college, where I studied psychology and writing, I became immersed in Miami's music and visual art communities, and started writing about the work my friends were making because it felt like the best way to witness and support it. Local journalism provided a foundation for my work; I became more curious about the folks I didn't know, and sought to connect with them through interviews. Photography was and still is a major part of my own practice, and everything became interconnected—it felt collaborative to speak with people, photograph them, and find ways to give them other platforms.

Being in Miami—a city in which the ecosystem of arts writing is still finding an infrastructure that can support it—opened up opportunities I likely wouldn't have had if I'd lived elsewhere. I feel grateful that covering the arts here eventually gave me the space to write about other topics I hold dear to my heart, which have been varied enough to make it difficult for me to find my niche: I write about film, video games, Florida history, my own ancestral heritage, and, especially, the changing environment, as it affects Florida and the world. They create a kind of web, with both art criticism and the interview format at its center. I am mostly guided by my curiosity about a subject, the feeling of writing *to* them; the spirit of collaboration is important to me, but so is solitude. Writing is messy, confusing, and often frustrating; touching on slippery topics can be hazardous. Still, it is my favorite way to learn.

WENDY VOGEL

I am a writer, critic, educator, and independent curator living in New York. I earned my undergraduate degree in French, with a minor in art history, from New York University. I then worked at the Museum of Modern Art as the assistant to a prominent curator. While studying for an MA in curatorial studies at Bard College, my lifelong interest in writing reemerged in courses taught by the former *New York Times* critic Michael Brenson and curator/academic Johanna Burton. My thesis-writing mentors Tirdad Zolghadr and Jenni Sorkin further guided my development of a feminist approach to criticism. After graduating from Bard at the height of the recession in 2009, I participated as a Critical Fellow in the two-year Core Residency Program at the Museum of Fine Arts Houston. There, I began my work as a freelance critic and adjunct instructor. My first bylines included Critics' Picks for *Artforum*; the late, great Texas art magazine *Art Lies*, under the editorship of Anjali Gupta; and the Austin-based art blog *... might be good*, where I held my first editor position from 2010–11. I then went on to edit at *Flash Art International*, *Modern Painters*, and *Art in America*. Today, my writing aspires to uphold a feminist legacy of criticality, intersectionality, and self-reflexivity.

EMILY WATLINGTON

Like many in the arts, I was good at drawing as a kid. And in my working-class Southern hometown, drawing and painting was the only art most people knew. Some dumb luck in the form of a scholarship made pursuing something as impractical as a BFA seem maybe worth the risk. When I got to art school, my mind was totally blown, and my favorite part was critique day. It didn't matter whether the work we were discussing was mine. In fact, I found being tasked with creating anything I wanted pretty daunting. As a first-year student—and still today—I preferred instead responding to others' prompts. I was also eager to find a source of income in a field other than fast food (it was exhausting, and I'm a vegetarian). So I convinced the museum affiliated with my college to make up a work-study position for me: curatorial assistant. It wouldn't cost them anything, I told them. The women who worked there were extremely supportive and let me write some of the wall and catalogue texts. I guess I've been writing ever since. *Art Papers* was the first place I published as a critic, and also where I guest-edited a Winter 2018/2019 themed issue on disability. Now I'm senior editor at *Art in America*—the magazine my high school art teacher had in her classroom.

LINDSAY PRESTON ZAPPAS

I started art writing as a young artist as a way to connect with other creative practices. I loved having the opportunity to peel back a curtain and dive into an artist's workflow and motives. Relationships with other artists and conversations held over beers after art crits were foundational in cementing my view of art criticism as something multivalent, mutable, and personal. That personal voice has always remained at the center of my work and of the criticism that I edit and publish—I look for art writing that cuts to deeper truths about humanity and connectivity. That is also a good way, I've found, to champion the diverse viewpoints of my writers. As an editor, my role is one of collaboration; the sharpening, honing, and refining that an editor contributes to the writing process allows for behind-the-scenes conversations to unfold with every writer. I highly value these hidden conversations and debates that take place in Word drafts and over emails—the discourse that the writing elicits before it is ever even published.

FURTHER READING

We asked contributors to share texts that were formative for their practice. We added pieces that informed and inspired this book.

Taylor Renee Aldridge, "Black Bodies, White Cubes: The Problem With Contemporary Art's Appropriation of Race," *Art News*, July 11, 2016.

Karen Archey, "Hack Life," *Art Papers* 37, no. 6 (November/December 2013).

James Baldwin, "If Black English Isn't a Language, Then Tell Me, What Is?," *New York Times*, July 29, 1979.

Andrew Berardini, "In Praise of Good Art Writing," *Momus*, January 6, 2015.

Elizabeth Méndez Berry, "Why Cultural Critics of Color Matter," *Hyperallergic*, May 3, 2018.

Elizabeth Méndez Berry and Chi-hui Yang, "The Dominance of the White Male Critic," *New York Times*, July 5, 2019.

Hannah Black, Ciarán Finlayson, and Tobi Haslett, "The Tear Gas Biennial," *Artforum*, July 17, 2019.

Brian Dillon and Boris Groys, "Who Do You Think You're Talking To?," *Frieze*, March 12, 2009.

Geoff Dyer, ed., *Selected Essays of John Berger* (New York: Vintage, 2003).

Mayanthi Fernando, "Critique as Care," in *Critical Times* 2, no. 1 (April 2019).

"For the attention of Philip B. Corbett, associate managing editor for standards at *The New York Times*," February 15, 2023, https://nytletter.com.

Hal Foster, "The Artist as Ethnographer," in *The Return of the Real: The Avant-Garde at the End of the Century* (Cambridge, MA: MIT Press, 1996).

Freelance Solidarity Project, https://freelancesolidarity.org/.

Orit Gat, "Art Criticism in the Age of Yelp," *Rhizome*, November 12, 2013.

Olivia Gauthier, "A Feminist Reckoning," *Art in America*, April 2019.

bell hooks, *Art on My Mind: Visual Politics* (New York: New Press, 1995).

Anthony Huberman, "Take Care," in *Circular Facts*, eds. Mai Abu ElDahab, Binna Choi, and Emily Pethick (Berlin: Sternberg Press, 2011).

Jamaica Kincaid, *A Small Place* (New York: Farrar, Straus and Giroux, 1988).

Jane Kramer, *Whose Art Is It?* (Durham, NC: Duke University Press, 1994).

Charlene K. Lau, "Resist the List: A Problem of Politics in the Evaluation of Contemporary Art," *C Mag,* May 31, 2013.

Ursula K. Le Guin, *A Wizard of Earthsea* (Berkeley, CA: Parnassus Press, 1968).

Sarah Lehrer-Graiwer, ed., *Pep Talk 5: Bruce Hainley* (Los Angeles: Pep Talk, 2011).

Sarah Lehrer-Graiwer, ed., *Pep Talk 7: The Rhonda Lieberman Reader* (Los Angeles: Pep Talk, 2018).

Lucy R. Lippard, *From the Center: Feminist Essays on Women's Art* (New York: Dutton, 1976).

Lucy R. Lippard, *The Pink Glass Swan: Selected Feminist Essays on Art* (New York: New Press, 1995).

Janet Malcolm, *Forty-One False Starts: Essays on Artists and Writers* (New York: Farrar, Straus and Giroux, 2013).

Kobena Mercer, *Welcome to the Jungle: New Positions in Black Cultural Studies* (New York: Routledge, 1994).

Michelada Think Tank, "A Teaser: A PoC Guide to Thrive," Issuu, February 9, 2016.

Helen Molesworth, "Amy Sillman: Look, Touch, Embrace," in *Amy Sillman: One Lump or Two,* ed. Helen Molesworth (New York: Prestel, 2013).

Toni Morrison, *Playing in the Dark: Whiteness and the Literary Imagination* (Cambridge, MA: Harvard University Press, 1992).

Brian O'Doherty, "Notes on the Gallery Space," in *Inside the White Cube: The Ideology of the Gallery Space* (Berkeley: University of California Press, 2010).

Sandeep Parmar, "A Q&A with Sandeep Parmar: Supporting Emerging Critics of Color," Poets.org, January 23, 2019.

Adrian Piper, "An Open Letter to Donald Kuspit," in *Real Life* 17–18 (Winter 1987–88).

Adrian Piper, "Power Relations within Existing Art Institutions," in *Institutional Critique: an Anthology of Artists Writings*, eds. Alexander Alberro and Blake Stimson (Cambridge, MA: MIT Press, 2011).

Yvonne Rainer, *Feelings Are Facts: A Life* (Cambridge, MA: MIT Press, 2006).

Adrienne Rich, "When We Dead Awaken: Writing as Re-Vision," in *College English* 34, no. 1 (October 1972).

Seph Rodney, "Reflecting on the Mistakes I've Made as an Art Critic," *Hyperallergic*, May 29, 2020.

Mira Schor, Emma Amos, Susan Bee, Johanna Drucker, María Fernández, Amelia Jones, Shirley Kaneda, Helen Molesworth, Howardena Pindell, Collier Schorr, and Faith Wilding, "Contemporary Feminism: Art Practice, Theory, and Activism—An Intergenerational Perspective," in *Art Journal* 58, no. 4 (Winter 1999).

Christina Sharpe, "Kara Walker's Monstrous Intimacies," in *Monstrous Intimacies: Making Post-Slavery Subjects* (Durham, NC: Duke University Press, 2010).

Gertrude Stein, *How to Write* (Paris: Plain Edition, 1931).

Sylvia Wynter, "Rethinking 'Aesthetics': Notes Towards a Deciphering Practice," in *Ex-iles: Essays on Caribbean Cinema*, ed. Mbye Cham (Trenton, NJ: Africa World Press, 1992).

ACKNOWLEDGMENTS

We would like to acknowledge the many collaborators who have nourished and contributed to *Track changes: a handbook for art criticism*. This publication would not have been possible without the support of Critical Minded and their executive director, rashid bumbray-shabazz, as well as the Rubin Foundation, the William Talbott Hillman Foundation, A.I.R. Gallery, and SOHO20. Thank you to everyone at the n+1 Foundation and Paper Monument for bringing this publication to life, including Dushko Petrovich, Roger White, Rachel Ossip, Dani Oliver, Dayna Tortorici, Mark Krotov, Nicole Lipman, Bryne McLaughlin, Judith Gärtner, and Vivien Anders. Most importantly, we want to thank each of the writers and editors featured in the book for inspiring this project and dedicating their time and work to its publication. Mira Dayal would like to thank Katie Giritlian, beck haberstroh, and Nicole Kaack for offering conceptual and editorial support, as well as the editors of *Artforum,* especially Isabel Flower, Michelle Kuo, and Elizabeth Schambelan, for providing mentorship and modeling editorial relationships. Josephine Heston would like to thank Sunny Leerasanthanah for offering constant encouragement and guidance.

COLOPHON

PAPER MONUMENT
Paper Monument is published by the n+1 Foundation, a nonprofit literary organization and the publisher of *n+1 magazine*.

Paper Monument
37 Greenpoint Avenue, Suite 316
Brooklyn, New York 11222
papermonument.com

EDITORS
Dushko Petrovich and Roger White

ASSOCIATE EDITOR
Prem Krishnamurthy

DESIGN
Judith Gärtner and Vivien Anders

ORIGINAL DESIGN CONCEPT
Wkshps

COPY EDITOR
Bryne McLaughlin

PROOFREADER
Emily Votruba

Track changes was published with significant support from Critical Minded. Additional support was provided by the William Talbott Hillman Foundation, the Rubin Foundation, SOHO20, and A.I.R. Gallery.

Paper Monument is supported, in part, by public funds from the New York State Council on the Arts with the support of the Office of the Governor and the New York State Legislature, as well as by public funds from the New York City Department of Cultural Affairs, in partnership with the City Council.

Track changes: a handbook for art criticism

ISBN 978-1-7365079-1-9
Printed in the United States of America
First printing